PROJECT SEMICOLON

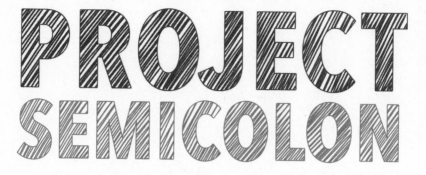

PROJECT SEMICOLON

your story isn't over

WITH **AMY BLEUEL**

FOUNDER OF THE SUICIDE-AWARENESS
ORGANIZATION THAT HAS HELPED MILLIONS

HARPER

An Imprint of HarperCollins*Publishers*

Project Semicolon: Your Story Isn't Over
Text copyright © 2017 by Amy Bleuel

Library of Congress Cataloging-in-Publication Data
Names: Bleuel, Amy, author.
Title: Project Semicolon : your story isn't over / Amy Bleuel.
Description: First edition. | New York, NY : HarperCollins, [2017]
Identifiers: LCCN 2016053515 | ISBN 9780062466525 (hardcover)
Subjects: LCSH: Project Semicolon (Organization)—Juvenile literature. |
    Suicide—United States—Prevention—Juvenile literature. | Mental
    illness—United States—Juvenile literature. | Self-help groups—United
    States—Juvenile literature.
Classification: LCC HV6548.U5 B54 2017 | DDC 362.28092/273—dc23 LC record available
at https://lccn.loc.gov/2016053515

Typography by Ellice M. Lee
17 18 19 20 21   PC/LSCH   10 9 8 7 6 5 4 3 2 1
❖
First Edition

To all those we have lost to suicide

WARNING: If you suffer from suicidal ideation or mental illness, some of the stories that follow may trigger an adverse reaction. If you feel this kind of content may be triggering, we advise that you consider not reading this book. And if you do read and a story is beginning to upset you, please stop reading it immediately.

For resources on getting help, please refer to page 329 in the back of the book.

FOREWORD

Loss from suicide is incredibly difficult to understand—from the questions that seem to have no answers to the pain that seems to have no end. More than one million times every year, friends and families of suicide victims struggle to comprehend why and how such a tragedy has found them. It was this loss, those questions, and that pain that inspired Amy Bleuel to start the suicide-awareness organization Project Semicolon in 2013. She wanted to invite the possibility of change.

Project Semicolon is a testament to what happens when one girl speaks up and tells her story. And Amy's story went on to inspire millions to lend their voices to one of the world's most troubling epidemics. The semicolon was chosen because, in literature, a semicolon is used when an author chooses to continue a sentence rather than end it. You are the author and the sentence is your life; you are choosing to continue. This book is filled with examples of people who chose not to end their sentences.

The semicolon movement has captivated the world, building a stage of courage where people in pain are encouraged to speak up. This is a movement that gives hope to those who question the value of tomorrow. *Project Semicolon: Your Story Isn't Over* is the embodiment of what Project Semicolon means. With a combination of stories and photos, it empowers those struck with tragedy to share their journeys. It is our hope that many will find themselves in these pages and realize *my story isn't over yet*. With this book, we want to continue spreading our important message of hope and love. The more people who learn that they are not alone in their struggles, the more lives we can save.

–PROJECT SEMICOLON

AMY BLEUEL

Life is full of trials that may bring a person great pain or, if they're lucky, great joy. We carry those experiences, the good and the bad, through life with us. They not only shape and change who we are, they also leave us with the lessons we have learned.

Growing up, for me, was one trial after another. I spent years wondering what I would eventually learn from my experiences and why I had to endure such horrible things. At some points, I even wondered if there could be a way out. From a young age, I had to learn how to endure and fight. At the age of six, two years after my parents divorced, I chose to go live with my father and his new wife in

Arizona. Living with my father was great until my stepmother began abusing me physically, mentally, and emotionally. I endured her abuse until I was taken from my father and put into the juvenile justice system and then a shelter home after I hit my stepmother back in self-defense. I remained there while I waited for my mother to come for me—which would end up taking a couple months. This happened at the age of eight, marking the start of my journey in "the system."

As a young child, I'd already experienced more pain than I imagined possible. Going forward with my life was difficult because of the years I'd been abused. I'd been left with a tendency toward seeking unhealthy kinds of attention and a habit for choosing paths that weren't beneficial for my life. I would get into trouble with the police for petty crimes and lash out in much anger to those whom I felt threatened by. I instilled much fear in the ones I loved through many violent outbursts. I would never physically hurt anyone other than myself, but there were many times those around me feared I would hurt them.

When I was thirteen, I entered back into the Wisconsin Juvenile justice system. The next five years of my life were spent in darkness and total solitude. I was heavily medicated with drugs used to treat mental illnesses, despite never being diagnosed with one. I fell victim to self-injuring behavior more than once: cutting, burning, head banging, and pulling out my hair. And, on a number of occasions, I even attempted to take my own life.

I had little to no respect for myself and felt that I was worthless. The people around me, especially those who were supposed to love me, never showed me that I was even worth the air I breathed. Their attitude about me became *my* attitude about me, and the mentality with which I viewed myself.

At the age of eighteen, I lost my father to suicide while I was still in the Wisconsin justice system. I had been at a low point for quite some time, but this brought more pain to my life than anything I had ever experienced. With that pain still lingering in the shadows, I was sent off to begin my life as an adult. I was fresh out of the criminal justice system and completely unaware of where or how to begin my life as an adult. So at that point, after five years of not being in school, I obtained my High School Equivalency Diploma and went off to college at the University of Wisconsin–Marathon County in Wausau, Wisconsin.

Beginning college brought an entirely new set of trials to my life. I started experimenting with drugs, which led me to abuse prescription painkillers. I also struggled greatly with depression during that period, which reflected very poorly on my performance in school.

Throughout my life, through the good times and the bad, I held closely to my faith in God. There were times that I wavered in my faith and wondered why I had to experience such pain, and times when I wondered how a God of love could allow me to go through this.

Meeting my husband at the age of twenty-five was the turning point in my life. For the first time, I experienced true love and was finally able to start healing. It was through this journey that I embraced my calling and set out to help others who felt they were less than their true worth. I knew I wanted to impact the world and to make a difference, which is how Project Semicolon started. I began

Project Semicolon to honor my father and to tell my story. I wanted to instill hope and love in others who also may have struggled or were still struggling in life. Project Semicolon began on April 16, 2013, by launching a graphic on the internet asking those who had struggled with mental illness or had lost a loved one to mental illness to draw a semicolon on their wrist and post a picture to social media, using our hashtags #ProjectSemicolon and #SemicolonProject416. The idea of Project Semicolon was developed through what I refer to as a perfect storm: God had given me something I would later develop into a movement that would reach millions of people.

Despite much heartache and pain I was able to rise from the ashes and prove the best is yet to come. It is my prayer that those who are struggling know that they are loved and that their stories matter. Whatever is happening to you in this moment, know that it does not define your worth. You can conquer the obstacles laid before you and come out stronger on the other side. You got this! I am right here cheering you on along the way.

Stay strong. Love endlessly. Change lives.

Amy Bleuel passed away on March 23, 2017. This book serves as a tribute to her incredible work with Project Semicolon. Her story—and her memory—endures.

Brittany M.

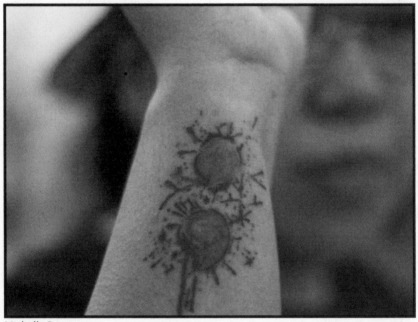

Michelle R.

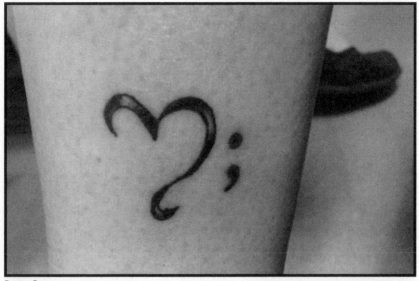

Dana C.

T.R.

ROS L.

I grew up with low self-esteem. I always thought I had to be skinnier, prettier, smarter—anything other than what I was—to fit in. I was the kid who wasn't invited to parties. I watched as my friends became popular while I simply faded into the background.

Maybe it was being alone for so long, or maybe it was because I didn't love enough, but I found myself crying a lot. When I look back at how I spent most of my high school days, it seems like I was always in a toilet stall crying. I just wanted to be like everyone else. I wanted to be happy, to feel liked, to be loved. Instead, I felt alone and unwanted.

When I was first diagnosed with depression in college, no one took it seriously. By senior year, I just couldn't cope anymore. My body ached, I skipped class, I slept all day and was a zombie at night. I hated taking the medication I was prescribed, so I stopped. It was a terrible idea; when I returned home after graduation, I tried to kill myself. I would have succeeded had my mom not come in and found me. She cleaned me up and made sure I survived the night. In the morning, I refused to talk about it because I didn't want to seem weak, didn't know how to explain depression to her. I still don't.

This year, I wanted to get off medication. I was feeling much better and wanted to feel "normal" again. But when I told my psychiatrist, I saw sadness creep into her eyes. She had come to the conclusion that I don't have severe depression. She diagnosed me with bipolar II disorder.

I don't know if I have come to terms with my diagnosis. I can't bring myself to tell my family or my friends. If anything, I want to run away and outrun the darkness that always seems to be near.

When I feel happy, is it real? Or is it just a moment of hypomania? I feel as though I cannot trust myself; I cannot trust the happiness I feel.

I'm scared, but I am hopeful.

JAYMEE B.

Someday, I'm going to change the world.

Today, I am a small-town twentysomething fighting a continuous battle with depression, anxiety, borderline personality disorder, and self-harm. I have been judged, dumped, left, and made fun of for this. But I've come to realize that there are a significant number of people who face a similar battle, and I want to connect with them. I want to force anyone who denies the reality of mental illness to accept those who struggle with it for how important they truly are.

MAUDE P.

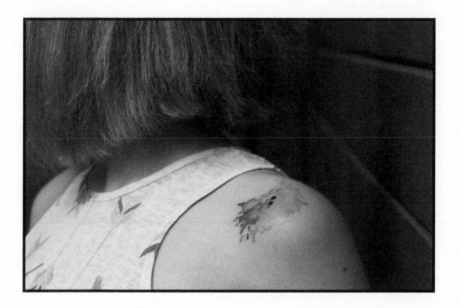

I am five years old. My heart aches every morning before going to school, and I get physically sick. Dad drives me, bowl and towel in hand. Odd, because I love school.

I am nine years old. The mystery isn't resolved, but it somehow disappears. Questions remain unanswered.

I am eleven years old. I can't do sleepovers without having to return home during the night because I feel such dire separation anxiety. I have difficulty adapting to change.

I am fifteen years old and a perfectionist. I am a bookworm, and I study all the time. Performance anxiety takes over. I compare myself to others; I always want more. More recognition, better grades, a brighter future. I am blamed for everything. I write everything down. My agenda looks like a novel. Not the kind you are proud of or that you would share; the kind that you hide because you are embarrassed about its existence and the hold it has on you. My agenda is my life; everything is written methodically. I am scared to death of forgetting to say or do something that could have an impact on someone around me. If I lose my agenda, my world will end.

I am seventeen. I just started college. Anxiety returns. In the middle of a class, my heart starts racing, my head spins in all directions, I have cold sweats, my body starts to itch and then goes numb. I can't breathe. My time has come. I'm going to die. This is the first of hundreds of panic attacks I will live through. I have three attacks a day. I feel like I've run a marathon after each and every one of them. I feel like I'm leaving my body each time it happens.

I am twenty years old. A special person in my life dies. Like that. One day here, the next day gone; no "good-bye," no "I love you." Everything within me breaks. The strong and determined young woman in me transforms into someone fragile and lost. I have no interest in anything.

I barely weigh one hundred pounds. It takes everything in my power to get out of bed. I have no energy for this battle. I develop an obsessive-compulsive disorder and overall anxiety issues. I quit school and stop working at the same time.

A short stay in a hospital allows me to meet with professionals who will help me to get better. I feel like a caged animal in that place. Like a disturbed person.

I decide to fight. To hold on to life. Because there is always that flicker of light at the end of the tunnel—as far and as small as it can be, it is there. Because life should be lived to the fullest. Because I am on this earth to accomplish something great and the best is always yet to come. Because I swear that in my darkest times, there was always a spark of hope and a breath of life.

M.P.

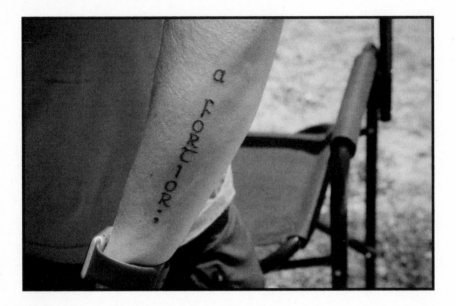

How do I tell a story that has never been told, to an audience I may never meet, to people who can judge me for the scars of my past? How do I tell that story? The truth is, it doesn't matter how I tell it, who is reading it, or who will judge me. It's my story, and I am sharing it to reaffirm that mental health issues do not discriminate. If my story offers hope to just one person, then my fear of stepping into the public eye for the first time, as a professional athlete and role model battling depression and anxiety, is worth it.

I am a professional hockey player in the National Women's Hockey League. But that is not where my story begins. My story begins on the University of Wisconsin campus in Madison, Wisconsin:

Waking up one morning to go to a team workout, swinging one leg after the other out of bed, I remember sitting up, both feet on the ground, looking at the dresser in front of me, thinking, *Why?* I had gotten to the point where getting out of bed was agonizing, where happiness wasn't an option because I didn't remember what it was. I spent the majority of each day thinking it would all be easier if I were gone. This is a mentality I never imagined I could have. Because I know the path of destruction that it leaves behind. I have seen it. Firsthand. When I was seventeen, my friend and teammate took her own life. I had never experienced grief like what I felt that day. Up until that point, I had been sheltered. I grew up in an area with a lot of money, in a family where I needed nothing and wanted for little. I lived in a massive house, my family drove fancy cars, and I had my school uniform dry-cleaned. I was a high school athlete with a full college scholarship, and my parents did everything in their power to protect that. I wasn't used to losing people, not like that. My parents couldn't explain it. I couldn't make sense of it. I didn't understand it. Until I found myself in Wisconsin, wishing I could end my own life.

For a few years I saw a therapist on and off. I took some medication, felt better for waves and then wouldn't again, but for the most part I thought it was behind me. Whatever was "wrong" with me, I could handle it. The worst was over. I could manage feeling sad, but the real darkness had disappeared. I was wrong.

After playing the maximum number of years of college hockey and exhausting my athletic eligibility, I still had some credits to finish up. I lived in an apartment alone, wasn't playing hockey anymore, and felt like I had completely lost control in my life. I could feel that heaviness start to creep back over me, but worse. I stopped leaving my apartment. Getting out of bed was torture, and every hour of the day I felt like I was repeatedly being punched in the stomach. I couldn't eat, couldn't sleep, would cry for hours, and I didn't understand why I couldn't just feel "normal" again. I didn't want people to think there was something wrong with me, so I isolated myself and didn't talk about it. I struggled every day to figure out what it truly meant to be happy, and despite looking everywhere, I couldn't find an answer. My parents told me to just wake up and put a smile on. They didn't understand that I couldn't change it. I was trapped in a darkness I couldn't escape and had no concept of how to find a way out.

Two days before graduation, I called home. I talked to my brother and my mom, and before I hung up I said, "I'm done." I got into my car, found an overpass, and drove full speed into the bridge. I woke up in the hospital, terrified of what I had done. Seeing the look on the faces of my family was the worst experience of my life.

I was lucky. Lucky that what I tried didn't work. Lucky that I have a family who has forgiven me. Lucky that I was given a second chance.

In my journey back from my accident, I have learned a lot. I have learned that the people I thought would judge me for my depression were upset that I didn't reach out. I have learned that my depression doesn't define who I am to the world. I have found the courage to finally be honest and open about my past. I was afraid of how the world would see me, afraid of the people I would let down and the stereotypes I would be subjected to in the athletic community.

I will undoubtedly face criticism for sharing my story. I will likely have people who try to use my past against me, and others who will unduly judge me, or simply try to be hurtful. I have learned that that doesn't matter. I am not less of a person because of the battles of my past, but rather, a better one.

What I have learned, most importantly, through my journey has been self-acceptance. I have accepted who I am as a person, entirely, and I live every day knowing that I am the most perfect possible version of myself. Over this past year I have become more comfortable talking about my personal experiences. I have opened up about my struggles. But this is the first time I am sharing my full story for the whole world to see. It is important to me. It is important because no matter who we are or where we come from, we all have demons. I am sharing my message because regardless of what light others may view me in, I still have days where I wake up and every step is a struggle. I am speaking out in the hope that others may come to terms in their own lives, and accept themselves completely for who they are. Mental health has no rules, knows no stranger, and can impact anyone. No one should ever try to walk that path alone.

KAREN V.

In Memoriam

There were many times Russ wanted us to break up so he would not be a burden to me, though I never saw it that way. Russ took prescription medications to treat his illnesses and they worked well enough, though the auditory hallucinations took their toll. It seemed he could never get rid of them no matter what he took or did. He informed me that the "voices" would put him down, tell him he was not good enough, berate him, and tell him other dark things. I did not always know how bad the dark things were for him because he would not confide in me, even when I became his wife; he did not want me to worry.

December 14, 2008, started out like any other Sunday. The weather had changed and the temperature was mild. Russ seemed a bit off that morning, but nothing he said or did concerned me. He went out to the garage to work on a project I later discovered he'd never started. When I went to check his progress and bring him in so we could get ready for church, I made the worst discovery anyone could: Russ had hung himself from the rafters.

He had seen his psychologist three days prior, and the doctor informed us after the fact that there were no signs of trouble, no indications that suicide was a thought in his mind. We—his family, friends, and the police—figured the voices told him to commit suicide in order to not be a burden to anyone. Months later, I found evidence in the browser search history on his computer that led me to believe he'd planned this day out.

I moved through the motions as a grieving widow. As the days and weeks passed, I found myself lost and confused, plagued with so many questions. Survivor's guilt followed me everywhere along with flashbacks, the inability to sleep, nightmares, night terrors, and emotional stress—all symptoms of PTSD, which I was later diagnosed with. I spent two years in counseling and in a few other programs and support groups working through my grief. My counselor told me, "You do not get over it; you work through it." I think of that phrase often.

On a retreat in Mexico, I finally accepted Russ's death and forgave God for allowing everything to happen. Russ left me with a special gift to help educate, inform, and inspire other people. Every October, we (the community, family, and friends) walk in the local Out of the Darkness Community Walk to raise awareness, educate about mental illness, and stomp out the stigma surrounding the completion of suicide.

My journey continues.

ALLY H.

My land legs are a bit wobbly as of late. Of course when I say *land*, I mean *life*, and when I say *wobbly*, I mean *vulnerable*. I am essentially feeling vulnerable in life.

Mayer-Rokitansky-Küster-Hauser syndrome (MRKH)—a condition that causes the vagina and uterus to be underdeveloped or absent—has been explained to me as a "genetic pothole in the road." And it has required a mammoth and grueling process of self-acceptance since I was diagnosed in my late teens. Being told at such a vulnerable and innocent age that you were born without certain "female parts" that instinctively and innately define us as "complete" women—despite on the outside looking "normal" (whatever that overused buzzword means)—was nothing short of harrowing.

Though this diagnosis no longer burdens me, the scars on my body do.

No one ever really stares or asks the uncomfortable questions. Friends say, "Could be anything—you could have fallen into something!" Yes, a razor blade!

Dark humor aside, I do see their kindness and I love them even more for wrapping me up in this beautiful and unconditional love. But frankly, I am really upset that I chose to brand myself in this manner. The process of self-acceptance rattled me in a way that I simply did not anticipate.

So, where to from here? I tackle this in the only ways I know how: I up my yoga practice, I swim alone, and I choose to be okay with that. I wear shorter sleeves on purpose and try to respond "thank you" to compliments. When I go on a date, I try to have twinkly eyes as opposed to internally rehearsing scripts of apology when my past is uncovered. Do I say I had a difficult teenage life? Do I say how I've come through the other side? Do I not say anything and wait for the question to be asked?

Only recently, I was walking to meet one particular boy for a Sunday afternoon of ocean frolicking and summer silliness. But as I approached the beach, I very nearly turned back. Why? Because there was a chance we might go for a swim. A swim! I would have to deliver my script, unclothe my past, absorb the stares, and risk a potential opportunity for love.

When did my fears become so profound that I would deny myself such precious moments? This is when I chose to change my script.

Self-harm is not attention-seeking or abnormal (as one date uttered under his breath at the end of a meal). It is not a weakness or a reason to be ashamed. My shame is stale and expired. For me, during that sad time, I was finding an expression when I didn't have the tools to express myself in any other way.

My expression was fear and a simple sadness at "not feeling good enough." I did this practice alone, quietly. I didn't understand it. I just know that when I do peer down at the scars that will never go away, I have an opportunity to embrace and love all that I am and all that I will become.

COLLEEN G.

My world has been falling down all around me since I can remember. But I guess when all your world does is fall, you quickly learn how to stand strong.

My early childhood consisted of me going back and forth between my divorced parents' houses. At my dad's, I got to watch him drink beer. At my mom's, I got to watch her sleep all day.

That was the year I learned loneliness.

When I turned five, I started kindergarten and was able to hang out with my cousins. Turns out one of my cousin's fourteen-year-old friends had a thing for little girls. He said if I told anyone, I would get in trouble. I didn't tell anyone.

That was the year I learned to be afraid.

At eight years old, I was a chubby kid. A couple of the boys would pull on the straps of my training bra and snap them against my back. Other kids would laugh because I couldn't run the mile fast enough.

That was the year I learned to hate my body.

When I was ten, my mom decided to move to another state. She left me with my dad, who was still drinking those beers all night.

That was the year I learned everyone leaves.

When I was twelve, I moved to my mom's house to give it a try. I had short hair and wore baggy clothes. All the kids in school called me a boy and spread rumors that I was bi. Every night I got at least five phone calls telling me, "Just kill yourself already." I moved back with my dad and the rumors started there too. Kids shoved me, spit on me, laughed at me, and made fun of me. Some girls tried to fight me while I ate my lunch.

That was the year I learned what a blade could do.

When I was fourteen years old, I started high school. I hung out with the upperclassmen to try to fit in. I started to date one of them. I fell in love with him. His friends decided they wanted me too. They touched me, hooted at me. He did everything he could to make them back off, but they just wouldn't listen.

That was the year I learned what it meant to want to die, the year I learned what depression is, what anxiety is. I learned that I have them. That was the year I learned that love can't heal you.

When I was sixteen years old, I had a friend. He and I hung out all the time. One night he stayed at my house like normal. I woke up with him on top of me. I puked and couldn't stop shaking.

That was the year I learned what rape was. That was the year I couldn't sleep without the lights on.

When I turned eighteen, I had a breakdown and didn't want to live anymore. I had to go to the mental hospital. I found out that I have PTSD from my rape. When I got home, my mom was wasted. She kept asking me why I didn't talk to her. I told her I just wanted to go to sleep. She yelled at me, said I was a liar, and kicked my fiancé and me out on the street at midnight. She texted me an hour later and told me not to "make a mockery out of suicide." My fiancé held me while I screamed and cried.

That was the year I learned what it felt like to shatter.

Now I am turning twenty.

This year I learned how to plan a wedding. I learned how to be a certified nursing assistant. I learned how to take care of myself. I learned the feeling of walking down the aisle. I learned how to love my husband more than anything.

I've learned a lot in this short life of mine. I've learned that life is very hard. Life is unjust. But I've also learned that if you know where to look, it's beautiful. I may have had a hard life. Some might even say an unbearable life, but now I wake up every day with a big smile on my face. I wake up knowing I have made it this far, so I can make it even further. I still have a lot to learn, and a rich, full life ahead of me.

NATASHA E.

All my life I have believed suicide was my only option for solving problems and dealing with feelings that seemed beyond me. I'm grateful that with a combination of one-on-one and group therapy, the right medication, finding a higher power, journaling, and lots of hard work over the last twenty years of my life, I have learned that I have more options than suicide. And I am stronger than I give myself credit for. I make life as simple as it can be and put my mental health above everything else; that is what keeps me carrying on.

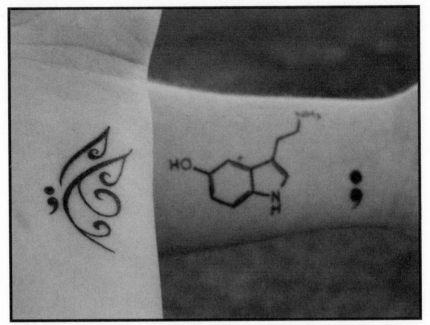

Christopher and Tabetha J.

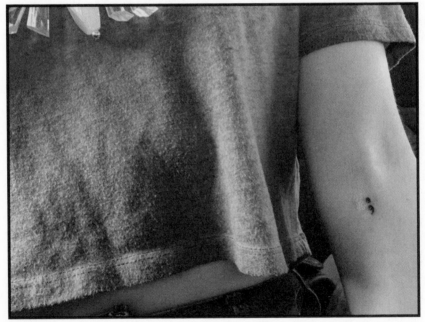

Alysa R.

Brittani S.

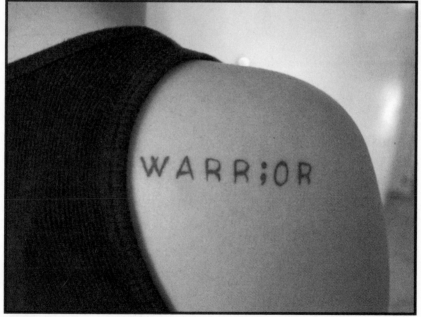

Chelsea B.

BRITTANY M.

I met my partner in 2008. We have been married for three years and I truly believe she was my saving grace. I am surrounded by her family and people who encourage and support me. I moved from America to Ireland to change my life and be with her. This was the best thing I ever did. Aine has taught me how to love myself and be the person I always wanted to be. That was something I had barely figured out how to do before it was all torn away from me because I was listening to the people who told me I would never amount to anything, and that I was stupid.

Now if I feel depressed I work on my photography. I love to tell stories of other people's lives and I love to help other people out. I've also begun to write again, this time about my life. I hope it will help me understand things better in the future.

HANNAH P.

I hated my therapist; she told my parents every time I told her about my self-harm. I hated that. I understand about my safety, but all she did was tell them, she didn't help me. So I just stopped telling her anything.

Things got better and seemed to stabilize for a few years, but eventually I found myself in a dark moment once again. I was becoming overwhelmed with my work, unable to focus, and unable to motivate myself. I saw myself going in a bad direction and started to panic. I scrambled to reach out for more support, but I already had a long history of feeling unable to talk about the real issues with my therapist.

Ultimately, to get the help I needed, I had to learn to advocate for myself and speak up for the kind of support I required. I found a new therapist and support group that have changed my life.

Everyone needs understanding—not just mental and personal insight, but also the insights of others. I know I have so much more to learn. I also know that I am very strong, and very smart. I won't forget the pain, suffering, and darkness. But most of all I won't forget how much I grew, how much I gained, and how strong I have become!

EMILY Y.

They told us drugs were everywhere. It was standard DARE programming, to tell us second graders to be wary of the substances lurking all around us. Although I knew how most drugs were ingested, I was convinced there might be drugs in the air outside or drugs on surfaces, so I refused to touch things outside. I didn't realize this wasn't normal until around the time I entered middle school. Suffice it to say, I was diagnosed with obsessive-compulsive disorder at a very young age.

To most of you, this will sound pretty irrational. It was. And although I eventually learned to handle OCD incredibly well, the stigma of it made me feel broken. I was constantly told that my thoughts were "wrong" and that I shouldn't feel the way I felt. I was told that I shouldn't tell anyone about my OCD because they would judge me. It created a lot of major insecurities for me that I didn't know how to deal with properly. I hated that "broken" part of myself, and thought other people would hate it too. As I got into high school and had my first boyfriend, I was terrified that no one could ever love me because of my OCD, that no one would ever accept me the way that I am. Because of this, I was constantly trying to change myself, to squash down my pain, to make myself a person someone could love.

As you can probably imagine, this led to several incredibly

unhealthy relationships. I let men tell me that my thoughts were wrong, that I shouldn't feel the way that I felt, and I let them blame me for the problems we had in our relationship. I let everything be my fault, so I was always the one apologizing. I felt terrible about myself. And even when I knew a relationship was toxic, I was terrified of being alone. I would break up with someone only to go back a few days later because I was so scared. I needed someone else to tell me that I was okay and to love me, because I couldn't love myself. In the times where the pain was too much for me to handle, I would hurt myself—cutting, literally hammering myself until I was black and blue, or exercising to an unhealthy extreme.

Despite all of this, I have somehow managed to be a (mostly) functional adult. I excelled at school and graduated college early. I didn't skip classes. I didn't party. I got a job immediately after graduation and have worked my way up for the past six years. I am a great worker, mostly because it's the only thing I've ever been good at, and it probably comes from my deeply rooted insecurities. I thought that if I could just be smart enough, or successful enough, then maybe I would have worth. This in itself created anxiety; if I made a mistake at work (which was rare), I would take it very hard and would be in a panicked state for about a week. My mind would go from "I made a small mistake" to "Oh my God, I'm going to get fired!" and I wouldn't be able to calm myself down. My mind would just spin and spin and spin.

When my boyfriend got a job in a different city, he asked me to move with him. My parents didn't want me to move, and at the back of my mind I knew that it probably wasn't the best idea. I did it anyway.

He was the only person I knew in that city, and I depended on him for so much. He was dealing with some of his own issues and didn't always treat me very well. But I loved him, so I moved. Our relationship quickly fell apart. I was a mess. I would have daily anxiety attacks waiting to hear from him each morning, I would cry on the bus ride home, I'd cut myself. I'd convince myself that it was my fault that he couldn't support me or be there for me. At the tail end of the relationship, I decided that my life needed to change and that I couldn't do it on my own. So I talked to my HR person at work, went on a leave of absence, and checked myself into the hospital that same day. That was the day my life turned around.

I spent five days in a psychiatric hospital with a team of doctors who helped me figure out a plan. When I transitioned to an outpatient program, I was still pretty touch-and-go. But by the end of the program, I had made a group of incredible friends who knew me, accepted me, and loved me for who I am. My psychiatrist also found me a therapist to continue with once the program finished.

I've been in and out of therapy since high school, but never found it super helpful. When I saw this new therapist, one of the first things she said to me was: "There's nothing wrong with you." I remember thinking, *What is wrong with this lady? Obviously there's something wrong with me. If there was nothing wrong with me, I wouldn't have hospitalized myself and I'd be happy.* Gradually, I came to understand what she was telling me. I came to understand that I felt so "wrong" because I believed I was broken. I believed that for a lot of reasons; that's what earlier doctors had told me, and through no fault of their own, that was what I experienced with my parents. It became a story that I told myself, but I could no longer recognize it as a story. I only saw truth. I took on their judgments and made them my own. But that year of therapy helped me realize how untrue (and how damaging) this story was and how it controlled me for twenty-five years. I realized there is nothing wrong with me; I am strong, resilient, brave, intelligent, and deeply empathetic. Yes, I have strong emotions, and that makes me different from a lot of people, but that doesn't make me wrong. I've come to see my differences as beautiful—the best, purest parts of myself.

RACHAEL K.

One day, I felt a little less happy than the day before, and the next day I felt a little less happy again, until one day, all my happiness disappeared. It stayed gone for a long, long time.

I was so empty and sad, none of my accomplishments in school meant anything. I still felt like a failure, never good enough. I hated myself with a passion, and felt I was a burden on everyone around me. I constantly told myself I was a tangible reminder of what everyone never wants to be. I was disgusted with myself, and was so depressed over my existence. I didn't want to live.

I reached a crisis point at nineteen and had to withdraw from university. I broke down emotionally; I spent my days and nights in bed, trying to block out the pain, just crying. Multiple suicide attempts followed, accompanied by never-ending helplessness and hopelessness and darkness. I was finally diagnosed with a severe episode of major depressive disorder, and admitted to a psychiatric clinic. Since that time, I have had thirty-six psychiatric hospital admissions, some lasting a couple of weeks, others up to a few months.

After an attempt on my own life that very nearly succeeded, I realized that although I didn't want to die, I just couldn't keep living the life I had been living for so, so long. I learned to wake up at some point in the morning, take my morning medication, achieve something little during the day such as going for a walk down the street (or to the letterbox), having a bath, or trying to watch TV in the evening, then take my night medication and go to bed. I went through the motions, even though I felt sad and depressed and ugly and awful. I did this for many months, just to survive. I learned that it was okay if the only thing I did that day was breathe. I told myself I was recovering from an illness, that I had to be gentle with myself and not blame myself.

I managed to go back to university, and earned an honors degree in psychology, specializing in the prevention of depression and anxiety in children and adolescents. It was extremely hard, and I achieved most of it from a psychiatric hospital bed. But I did it because I wanted something good to come out of all the pain I had been through.

I'm aware that my life will, in all probability, include relapses. That's okay. I've had to accept the fact that complete recovery will probably not be my reality, but I'm determined to enjoy a good quality of life, even if it isn't perfect. Even if it isn't what I expected.

What I held on to, and still cling to, is hope. Hope sustained me when I had nothing else. Hope can seem irrational in the face of darkness, but I am alive today because of hope. Because a little voice inside kept telling me that I would get through. And I did. I kept fighting again and again and again. Until finally, I felt it for the first time in so long: happiness and freedom. And it was worth every single step of the fight.

I celebrate life itself, the good things in the past, the things I'm letting go, and what I'm looking forward to experiencing in the future. I celebrate hope.

> *I celebrate being alive.*
> *I celebrate who I am.*
> *I thought I'd never be able to say that,*
> *but I can now, and I like it.*

DANIELLE C.

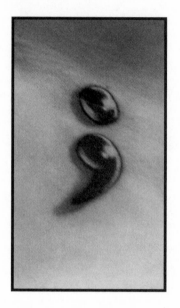

After developing anorexia at twelve years old, I was bullied in high
school for being small and skinny, and later on for being a lesbian.
I became very angry toward everyone, shutting myself away from
the world and starting to self-harm. Eventually, my depression and
anxiety became so bad that I tried to commit suicide twice. I finally
sought help and started seeing a counselor.

I didn't get my semicolon tattoo to show others; I use it as motiva-
tion. When I hit a low I look at it and remind myself that I can do this.
I can beat this darkness.

ANTHONY K.

I grew up in a violent household; my father was an abusive alcoholic. One of my first memories at the age of five was helping my mother barricade the bedroom as he chased us through the house with a chef's knife. Eventually I was put into a Catholic elementary school, where I thought I would be safe.

I was wrong.

I was bullied severely—physically and verbally abused—by my classmates from second grade all the way to senior year of high school. I began to self-harm when I was sixteen. While I never cut, I used to burn myself. In my twenties, I ended up dating a badly abusive woman who constantly told me I was useless, stupid, and worthless; she even filed false charges against me multiple times, resulting in my arrest and a three-night stay in jail. Over the years, I attempted suicide four times—all hangings.

I reached my lowest point and knew I needed to change my life.

I moved out of the place I shared with the abusive ex on Christmas Eve, and I decided to go back to school full-time. Graduation was one of the best days of my life. It's been six years since I've attempted suicide or any kind of self-harm, but that's not to say I haven't thought about it.

I have hope—hope for the future, knowing that my life is precious and has meaning, just like everybody else's.

ALICIA R.

Growing up with a mental illness, I often felt torn between two people. One was Public Me, the quirky manic pixie dream girl. The friend, daughter, student, sister, and overuser of hashtags and social media.

Private Me was different. I constantly battled personal villains like self-hate, anxiety, body issues, an eating disorder, depression, and suicidal ideation. I was always told these are things you don't bring out in public, to protect the people in your life from your feelings.

Like anyone with dual identities, I could only keep my two lives separate for so long. Eventually, they started to mix and I became someone my family, friends, teachers, and even I didn't recognize. It felt like I was losing to my personal villains, and I couldn't save the ones I loved from suffering at their hands, too. So, after many lost battles trying to keep my mental illness hidden away, I tried to take my own life.

It wasn't until a few days into my stay at a local hospital that I was helped by the best superhero I could ask for. She was a patient in the ward, an older lady who had been creepily looking at me for a few hours. She came over to me and said, "From one crazy person to another, you will need this." She put a necklace in my hand and wandered off. The necklace was a simple silver chain with one charm on it that said "Hope." With this simple action, she showed me that people with mental illness are human. That even though she was sick, she connected with me and helped me by giving back exactly what I'd lost. Hope that I could be a good person and an important part of society.

That sort of thinking opened up my mind. I realized that asking people with mental health issues to hide their struggles was like asking a superhero to fight off the worst bad guy with no weapons or superpowers. She showed me that people living with mental illness are incredibly strong, and that strength is something we should never try to hide. It's something we should celebrate. I was angered by the fact that the stigma around mental illness forces people to hide their strength; if we instead suffered from cancer, the world would be celebrating our will to survive.

From that point, I stopped being ashamed of living with a mental illness. I now try, instead, to be my own superhero. Even though I might not always make the right decisions or have the easiest journey, my story—and all our stories—are so incredibly valid. After all, you are still a badass superhero, even if the only person you ever save is yourself.

My truth is that mental illness still affects my life, which means I have amazing days and terrible days. Yes, some days are kicking butt at work and laughing with my friends. Other days, I binge-eat all my feelings and think about suicide. I share these experiences to show people that you can be both: an advocate and struggling; successful and depressed; imperfect and inspiring; and a role model while still trying.

By the age of eleven, I had stopped eating altogether. I was desperate for the bullying at school to stop. With every hurtful word that was said to me, I believed my bullies more and more. I believed I was ugly, fat, stupid, not "normal." The only way I could stand up for myself was to become the bully. I hurt people the way others hurt me. I became violent. I got into fistfights. I became a regular in detention and hated myself more and more for being who I was. I had no friends. Everyone was afraid of me. What did I have left to live for?

For some reason, self-harming was an instant release. If you ask other self-harmers, many of them will say the same thing. It immediately alleviated the intense emotions I was feeling when I didn't know how to handle them. My anger became uncontrollable, but cutting helped me calm down. The feeling of that razor blade against my flesh was the most comforting feeling I had felt in a while—so comforting, it became my best friend.

I was raised Catholic. I was taught that suicide was a mortal sin and would automatically damn you to hell for eternity. But my secret was becoming more and more overwhelming. By fifteen, I had attempted suicide twice. My thoughts of worthlessness took over and the slightest thought of happiness was pushed so far out of my mind, I didn't know what happiness was anymore. After graduation I experienced a lightning-fast decline physically, mentally, and emotionally. I became this empty shell of a human being. I didn't care if my impulsivity, drug use, or alcoholism killed me or not. I felt so worthless and was so careless with my life. I didn't care about anything anymore.

Around this time, the unimaginable happened. I remember the night so vividly that I still have nightmares about it to this day. I was hanging out with my best friend. We had a bonfire and her friend invited a bunch of his buddies over. I didn't know any of them. One guy especially was acting a little too friendly and made me very uncomfortable. I told him I wasn't interested. I was very intoxicated and should have gone to the hospital for alcohol poisoning. I went to the guest room to pass out for the night when this same guy forced his way into the room and locked the door. He pushed me down on the bed and told me if I screamed, he would kill me. I knew he had a gun because he had been showing it off earlier that night. All I could do was cry and keep saying "no" over and over and over until he pulled the gun out, put it to my head, and told me to shut up. He raped me for hours that night. My best friend was asleep in the room next door and to this day doesn't know what happened. I felt used, ashamed, and disgusted. The next day I sat in the shower fully clothed, crying my eyes out for hours.

After the rape, my suicidal thoughts were at a constant high. My eating disorder, drug use, self-harm, and suicide attempts became a daily struggle. I never left my bed.

Finally, I agreed to get the help I so desperately needed late last year. I went to a residential treatment facility where I was diagnosed with severe depression, PTSD, panic disorder, borderline personality disorder, severe anxiety disorder, OCD, dissociative disorder, insomnia, nightmare disorder, and body dysmorphic disorder. Finally an answer to why I feel the way I do and why I act the way I do. I met so many incredible women there who all had the same mental illnesses as me. I have been in recovery for almost a year and it has been the most difficult thing I have ever done. Yes, I still struggle daily and have suicidal thoughts, but asking for help and accepting my illnesses has been lifesaving.

To everyone who feels worthless, hopeless, and like you can't survive another day: I am living proof that you can. Recovery is possible. It takes hard work, but learning to live and love again is a process that unfolds one day at a time.

SADIE W.

I t started out really small when I was really small, just school trou-
bles, friend issues, and anxiety. But as I grew, so did this disease.

Despite all I had been blessed with, I never felt good about myself.
I never felt pretty enough, or popular, or smart, or like I could ever
have a boyfriend . . . the list goes on and on. Most everyone struggles
with these issues at some point, but to me the problems felt elevated
and put me in a dark state. I started to see a counselor and began
antidepressants in the fifth grade.

When high school started, things were good my freshman and
sophomore years. I played soccer on varsity, I had a few really good

friends, and I was always busy doing something. Then, my junior year, my brother and all his friends left for college, leaving me with few friends my own age. I broke my collarbone and had knee issues that caused me to lose the one thing I'd had since I was three: soccer. In February my best friend was arrested and kicked out of school, and one week before this my parents informed me they were getting divorced. I began to take my meds and visit my counselor again at my parents' request. I toughed out the rest of high school and decided going to a new state for college was the best thing for me.

Turns out, I was destined to repeat a similar pattern in college. My first semester was amazing: I had so many friends, a boyfriend, and a 3.6 GPA. Then came spring semester. I didn't make it into a sorority like all my friends, my boyfriend broke up with me, and my classes were getting harder. The depression came back, worse than ever before. I had suicidal thoughts nearly every week. I finished the semester and moved home, where my mom and I got me restarted on my medicine. I was happy again, finally. When I went back to school for summer classes, I was alone far too often, which led to a lot of overthinking. This resulted in me slitting my wrist one night, just wanting to end this terrible fight. My attempt thankfully failed, but I moved back home permanently and began to receive the help I so desperately needed.

Now I am working every day to be the best me and be happy. I'm not gonna lie, it's not always easy. Some days I just wanna lie in bed and cry. And every once in a while I do let myself cry and be upset. Because it is okay to not be okay sometimes. But I never let those dark days take over anymore. I know that God is greater than all my ups and downs, and He is not finished with me.

JANA A.

grew up with emotionally and verbally abusive parents. Sometimes physically, as well. Often I would go to bed without dinner, or with a new bruise, or with the echo of their voices saying that I didn't "get a vote." Once, my mother chased me down the hallway with a shoe. When I locked myself in my room, my father threatened to beat down the door and not replace it if I didn't come out to face them.

Things were worse when we moved to a new town. I had nowhere to escape to, no sleepovers every weekend. No neighbor whose house I could run to in the middle of the night. It was clear to me that my life meant nothing to my parents, and I could see no other way out. I picked a date and made a plan.

I don't remember most of that semester. Almost six months of my life are just darkness that I cannot see through. What I know for sure is that my best friends at the time saved my life; they are the reason I ended up not going through with it. I relapsed again my freshman year of college. I'd survived high school by thinking about how college would be my saving grace. Sadly, my roommates bullied me badly and after one day of being back with my parents for winter, the thought of suicide popped back into my head.

I am proud to tell people about the last ten years—how they almost did not happen, yet they did. About all of the incredibly tough times I faced and all of the wonder that came from it. Just last year, I spontaneously purchased a one-month ticket to Europe. I spent five months traveling around Europe, Israel, and the US, just living out of my giant backpack. In the last year, I have been to ten countries. I went camping for the first time. I had my first date ever. I traveled solo. I got my first job abroad. I finally separated from my parents and became independent. I have met countless wonderful friends.

No, not every day is easy. Some days I wake up and just feel as though I am in a funk. Everything feels off and my smile feels fake. Some days it's just a losing battle. I remind myself that it's good to be the sun, shining my light for others, but sometimes it's okay to be the sunflower—soaking up the light I can't make on my own.

Life is hard, but oh so beautiful, exploding with color.

KRISTINA F.

In Memoriam

When we got the call that my brother Keith had committed suicide, it felt like my world stopped. My heart was broken. I was lost and my emotions were uncontrollable. He was my only sibling, and we were so close. I felt immediately alone.

There were no signs the week before he passed. He was his usual active self who loved blasting his music and playing video games. What we found out after he passed is that he had spent the weekend away with an ex-girlfriend he'd been trying to reconcile with. Things did not go well, so he purchased a gun and died by suicide in a hotel room.

Alone.

Why didn't he call anyone? We were so close, I wish he would have called me. Why didn't he? That's a question I will always ask myself and one that can't be answered.

After his passing, my anxiety exploded. But with therapy and medication, I am coping. It will be a constant roller coaster of emotions, but will get better over time. There are times when I am okay, and there are times when I am not okay. I couldn't look at pictures or videos of Keith for a while, but now I embrace them and remember the good times. No one can take that away from me.

I truly believe he is at peace. I'm still here, and I do what I can to spread the word about suicide prevention and participate when I can to help end the stigma. The hurt and pain he caused to me and my parents has been devastating, but we are survivors and will forever love him. A piece of my heart remains with him. I am a stronger person with a more open heart, and I have learned that you cannot sweat the small stuff, there is no time for that. Love and live now, and continue to make memories . . . you are worth it.

STEPHANIE P.

Anxiety and phobias left me sleepless and tortured as a child. Though I saw a psychiatrist and took medication, my struggles led to my first suicide attempt at age eleven.

I developed chronic pain and seizures and, for most of my teenage and early adult years, I was in and out of hospitals. At one point when doctors could find absolutely nothing wrong with me, I wondered if I was crazy.

By 2010, I was living in pain about 90 percent of the time, and my daughter, who was just seven years old at the time, started to get very sick. Sick just like me, only her doctors immediately figured out what was wrong. Finally the puzzle was starting to form a picture: I gave my daughter the same brain condition I'd had all along, called Chiari malformation, as well as a connective tissue disorder called Ehlers-Danlos syndrome. That condition can cause severe chronic pain. We both ended up in brain surgery, as well as other surgeries and treatments.

People have absolutely no idea how many people commit suicide because of chronic pain. I still struggle with anxiety and PTSD; I don't go out in public often, but step by step I find myself completing one small goal at a time. I think a lot about how I tried to take my own life, when actually, there was this "thing" there all along trying to take it from me. It took me almost losing a life I had been given to appreciate the one I have.

KRYSTLE D.

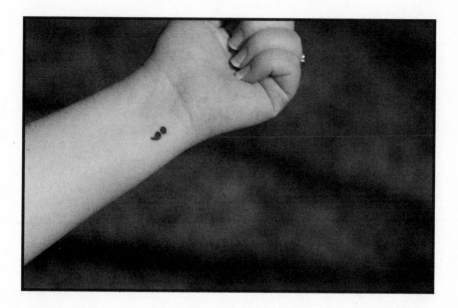

I remember sitting in the rocking chair, looking out the window. I remember hearing my husband talking to my therapist: "You think she's showing signs of postpartum?" he said. That's when I knew life was going to change.

Depression was not new to me. We had first been acquainted when I was just five years old, and my younger brother was diagnosed with a brain tumor. Doctors told my mother to make funeral arrangements because there was no way Kyle would survive. Understandably, my parents focused all of their attention on their sick son. But five-year-old me didn't understand why they couldn't call to check up on me at home, why no one was around to bring me to the park after school. I was lonely and scared. In some ways, I never stopped feeling that way.

Miraculously, Kyle got better. He has scars on his head, reminding us of that time. I carry the scars on my heart.

When my daughter was born, I had the normal first-time-mom jitters, and at some points just cried because she wouldn't latch, or she spit up after I'd just given her a bath. My husband and I were both tired from the nighttime feedings. But I was starting to feel extremely different and odd. I didn't know how to put it into words. After being diagnosed with postpartum depression (PPD), I was put on a high dose of lithium. I had to stop breastfeeding, and needed to focus on my treatment more than taking care of my daughter. My close family members took over and helped with the baby. I slept a lot, ate little, showered hardly at all, and cried constantly. I felt like I was suffocating. I kept thinking, as time went on, that my daughter was growing without me. I wasn't there to change her diaper or coddle her when she whimpered. I felt like a waste and couldn't handle interacting with anyone. I was in and out of the hospital for psychosis and suicidal thoughts. Looking back, I was so numb from the nine different medications I was taking daily that half of my daughter's childhood so far is a blur. Doctors tell me now that having another child should not be on my radar. I could be diagnosed with PPD again, and it could be even worse than the first time.

Three years have passed, and I still sometimes feel that pit in my stomach that reminds me of how it used to be. I still struggle with depression. I am currently titrating off some of my medications. I am proud to say that I cried a few months ago, something I hadn't done since my first few months of PPD.

I am so hopeful in my life that this will all change. I work hard at being proactive, positive, and keeping the faith. My daughter keeps me going at times when I am feeling my lowest, and my husband is my number-one supporter. Even though I still have panic attacks and bouts of depression, I would not have my life any other way.

I am not ashamed of who I am, what I have done in my life, or the things that have crossed my mind. I am proud of the person I am becoming and the life that I get to share with my daughter and husband.

JOSHUA S.

I was a normal kid: energetic, loud, hyper. I had lots of friends, and not much to frown about. I also had a physical disability, which meant I would have a challenging time doing things that most of my friends did seamlessly—sports, workouts, etc.

I started to adopt a belief that I was inferior because of the way I walked (I limp a little), and because of some of my mannerisms. This belief in my own inferiority was the groundwork for self-harm. Hurting myself was an escape from those feelings.

A few years ago, I pulled the trigger on a firearm that luckily was empty. This was my moment of awakening and revelation—the overwhelming feeling of regret for what I'd tried to do and gratitude that I was unable to do it.

I had to answer the biggest questions of my life: Who did I want to become in this world? How was I going to achieve that?

My life is overflowing with opportunities now—in my career, with my family, in my everyday life. Remember to live life as kings and queens. Make the kinds of decisions that serve humanity and consistently challenge you and everyone you come across.

Show the world what you've got.

LISA A.

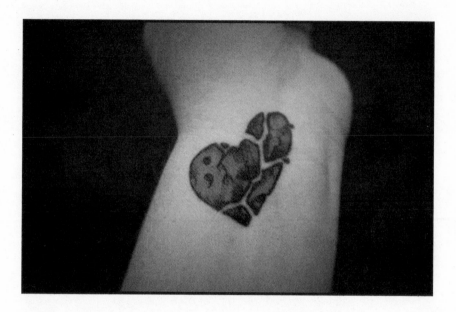

She was coming at me nonstop, so I pushed her.

She fell, and fell hard.

I'll never forget my father's face. The fear. Had I really hurt her? Would she get up? He whispered at me, "What did you do?" I stood there paralyzed, yet fully aware of the ramifications of my actions.

I had pushed her so hard she fell backward into the upstairs hallway right outside my bedroom door. Her head put a huge dent in the wall.

I stood above her, angry and over it. Over the beatings. I was sixteen years old. This had been life for many years already.

She had been at it for hours, lunging at me with her fists and slapping at my face. My blood was boiling over and I finally lost it. I chose to defend myself. I pushed back.

I stepped backward and shut my door slowly, leaving them lying in the hallway. I heard him talk softly to her as I slid down the back of my door and sat in a ball, shocked.

What damage had I done?

I just wanted her to stop hurting me. I wanted to escape.

It was late. I sat there for several minutes and waited to hear if she would get up and go, or if she would start up again, only twice as bad.

My father sat with her in the hallway and waited until she could move. It was suddenly quiet.

They left.

I decided to pull my bed over to my door and block it. I really wanted to go to sleep. Sleep was the only time I felt calm, though I was never able to sleep more than two or three hours at a stretch. The stress of that house had me always on edge, waiting for the next pounce.

We never discussed what had happened that night, and life went on like "normal." I cried almost every night, hoping I would survive long enough to get out of that house—that cold, dark, horrific house, filled with secrets and lies. The problem with my mother's alcoholism was that she blacked out and never remembered the beatings and torture she had doled out the night before. She slept it off and had no clue about the terror she unleashed at night. The loud music, the long lectures sitting at the kitchen table, the constant beatdowns, because we were her punching bags. My father took it, my brother took it, and I took it, day in and day out. When darkness fell outside, her rage dawned inside.

At my lowest I decided death would stop all the pain and suffering. So I planned my suicide.

I hung the rope. Closet door wide open. Chair set. I stood there and stared at it. In my head I watched myself die. Suffering no longer, and the weight of this battered life no longer weighing me down. I saw myself light as a feather, floating up, up, up through the sky, seeing pretty fluffy clouds, a bright sun, and God's hand reaching for mine. As I moved closer, I would feel free and all pain would cease. He would wrap Himself around me and finally it would be over. Pain would stop. I prayed every night that God would protect me. I believed then and still believe now.

I stood there. Silent. Minutes passed. Then an hour. I sat quietly on my bed and lost the courage to do it. Killing myself was much harder than I had imagined. I shut the closet door and lived to tell my story.

I live with a broken heart, but I love with the whole thing—through the cracks. I find something every day to be thankful for. I refuse to let what happened to me define me as a wounded person; instead it defines me as a warrior who battles every single day to love her life, no matter the struggle.

BRIAN H.

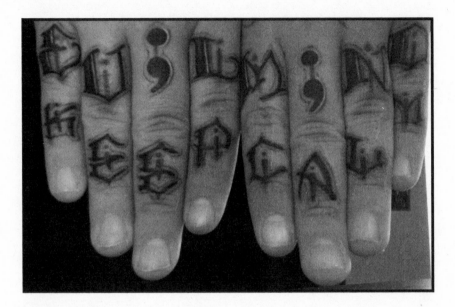

My parents started taking me to see a psychiatrist when I was twelve. I was always told to take the medications I was on for depression, anxiety, bipolar, and mood disorders, but being young and not having any education about what I was dealing with, I lied to my parents and told them I was taking my meds.

In high school, I got involved with Xanax, Ecstasy, and LSD. They were my escape from reality, a way for me to forget about the family issues and the problems I was dealing with.

After a very unfortunate car accident that could've taken my life plus other innocent lives, I realized that my addictions were a serious matter. I wanted help and finally realized it was time to get right. I did my own reading and realized this was a disease I would have to face to overcome. Running away to drugs wasn't going to help.

LEXI C.

They told me in fifth grade I had depression. I remember my mom blowing it off, like it was nothing. I tried to kill myself for the first time a year later. *What could possibly be so bad in a sixth grader's life that she'd want to die?* Let's just say I wouldn't wish the home life I had on my worst enemy.

In high school, I met a guy who literally tortured me daily. He would say horrible things to me and about me every single day, in every class that we had together, in front of everyone. The teachers and the administration looked the other way since his mom was a teacher. To this day, I still have no idea what I ever did or said to make the guy act so cruelly to me. I ended up dropping out of my public school six weeks into my junior year. I just couldn't take it anymore. I stayed out of school for the remainder of the semester and enrolled at an alternative high school. It had a bad reputation but I loved it there. The teachers and staff really cared about every kid who walked through the door.

I thought I was a pretty good kid up until I turned seventeen. I started smoking weed with my friends, and soon developed a pill addition. That led to cocaine and worse. There are parts of my life I have zero recollection of.

One thing I do remember is being raped at a friend's house on

Easter Sunday. I was a virgin. I never turned him in or talked about it afterward; I was embarrassed about it and I didn't want to take the risk of somebody blaming it on me.

I've been hurt so much in my life, by everyone I've ever loved. It's made me very guarded and very closed off to any sort of vulnerability. I don't let people in. I have a lot of friends, but I would say that none of them actually know the real me. I was determined never to give anyone a chance to hurt me, but then . . .

I met him.

I had never felt so intensely about someone or had such a passionate relationship with another person so fast. Maybe that was a warning. Maybe that's why it hurt so badly when he broke up with me very unexpectedly. He screamed and said things to me that still hurt me to this day. His words cut deep; he knew how to hurt me. And he did. I was destroyed. My depression got worse and worse.

Last fall I was literally at my breaking point. I didn't care if I lived or died. I thought about killing myself often. My best friend from college had been telling me for months that I needed to tell my doctor, because she could help me. I didn't know how to even start that conversation. It's so hard for me to admit "weakness."

I finally took her advice and I sat down and talked to my doctor about it. Instead of having a ten-minute visit, she sat and talked to me for an hour. I feel very alone most of the time, so to have somebody sit down and listen to me talk about my problems and how they affected my life meant everything to me. I credit my doctor and my best friend for saving my life.

I wish that I could say that my life is turned around now. I wish that I could tell you that things were perfect and I'm a happy person. But the truth is that I still struggle daily. I have been diagnosed with major depressive disorder, general anxiety, and panic disorder. There are days when it's hard for me to get out of bed. There are days when I *can't* get out of bed. There are times when I just want to sit in my house and be alone. I guess I'm lucky that I have good friends. The ones who don't give me "the look"—and you know exactly the look I'm talking about. It's the one from people who completely don't understand what you're going through and can't offer you any empathy.

What I want everyone to know is that the sun is going to rise tomorrow whether you want it to or not. Life is tragic, but it's also beautiful. I'm still here and I'm still fighting and, thankfully, I have people ready to fight for me when I can't.

F.F.

For as long as I can remember, I have been depressed—different and overall awkward in general. Unpopular, not pretty like the other girls, with a big ol' dark-blue birthmark covering my left eye that looks like I got punched. I have never had many friends and was moved around a lot when I was a kid. When I was nine years old, I was put into foster care and got out when I was seventeen due to irreconcilable differences with my last foster mother. For three years, all I did was work, party, and jump from relationship to relationship. It was a tumultuous time. One of those failed relationships ultimately led me to Florida.

I feel like I was completely naïve until I had to take a job as a cocktail waitress at a strip club. I learned a lot there: how to be conniving, how to hustle, and how to hold in the tears when I got passed over for a hotter girl. This especially took a toll on me a year later when I decided that dancing would bring in better money. It was great for a while, until other people in my life found out about it and treated me badly because I was living "that life."

One night while I was out, I shattered my foot and had to be stuck in the house with no way to work or pay bills, leaving me with a big decision to make. That decision was whether to start college. I was twenty-three at the time and had been working in a pharmacy for a couple of years. I always had my bosses and family urging me to make a better life for myself. They knew I had potential. So I worked and went to school and four years later, received my associate of arts degree.

I was in the final year of a PharmD program when a six-month fast-track relationship sent me spiraling into the most depressed state I had ever been in. By the time we broke up, I had been going through medication after medication to try to control my anxiety.

I was going to my psychologist weekly and my psychiatrist monthly for more med changes. I literally experienced every single side effect from antipsychotic and antianxiety medications there is: extreme weight gain, psychotic breaks, mood swings, and suicidal behavior. The fourth time I tried to end my life, I woke up three days later with a migraine that wouldn't quit and I just remember lying there crying because I was so mad that I didn't die, and because no one even noticed that I'd disappeared for that long. I was living in a nightmare. To add to it, I was getting into trouble with school, and my family did not seem to understand what I was going through. I fear they may never forgive me for failing my third year.

I just finished "third year squared," as I call it, after repeated appeals to my program administrators won me a second chance. I have always managed to make it through life's trials, and I am determined to see this through to the end.

Living with mental illness and not being able to just settle in life is the most exhausting thing I can think of, and there are more days than not when I want to just stay in bed and sleep my life away. But more than that, I want to make my own future. It's important that other people who struggle do the same. Life is not going to be great every day, but it helps to know we're not alone.

Christy B.

WARR;OR

April J.

Carrie G.

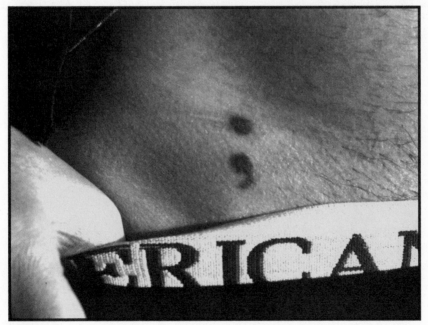

Benjamin P.

HEIDI R.

My first boyfriend abused me. He would hit me, and he would tell me that no one wanted me—no one but him. Therefore he was allowed to treat me like absolute crap.

But I found my strength. I ended the relationship. I stopped cutting. Today I am proud of myself, because I'm the one who got me through the dark and back to the light.

KIMMY T.

In Memoriam

The day my sister chose to end her life changed me forever. Her suicide left me alone, frightened, and drowning in a sea of darkness. Suicide ended a pain she was suffering in silence and caused me immeasurable agony. I thought about doing what she did. Just end the sleepless nights filled with wondering why she chose this and how I had failed her. Missing the signs. Classic survivor guilt. But something stopped me. Ironically, it was my sister. She had always been my biggest supporter and I knew if I killed myself, she would feel responsible. It made no sense yet it made all the sense in the world to me and probably saved my life.

She wanted me to follow my dreams and passions. She told me I could do anything. Her suicide note said so.

When I stumbled upon Project Semicolon, it moved me in ways I'm not sure I can articulate. It's exactly what my sister was telling me in her last words to me. Finish my story.

The more we reduce the stigma attached to the word *suicide* and encourage discussion about depression and mental health, the more lives will be saved. I got a semicolon tattooed on my foot as an everyday reminder that someone loved me enough to make me want to finish my story.

That someone was my sister.

NINA M.

In Memoriam

My only sister left us on April 17, 2015. But it was not the Hope we all knew and loved who left us; it was someone else. Something had stolen our Hope from us. It was depression, sadness, and loneliness mixed with things she believed could numb her pain, make it go away.

My sister could light up a room and she never met a stranger. She was well respected in her profession and affected so many lives in a positive way with the work she did. She seemed to always have a smile on her face, but underneath, the sickness was winning.

Those of us left behind can't help but wonder, Why? Why didn't I see this? Why didn't I help stop it?

Losing a loved one to suicide is more difficult than words can describe. We as survivors have to put the pieces of a lot of unanswered questions together. We do this to try to find some clarity and reasoning for this tragedy. At the same time we have to keep all the good things alive for her children. Telling the kids their mom was happy makes it hard to explain why she's not here. When the time comes, hopefully they'll understand.

I truly wish I could wake up from this nightmare, but this is reality. It hurts like hell and I hate depression for leading my sister down a path she could not come back from.

Do what needs to be done to stay. Counseling, psychiatry, medication, rehab . . . whatever it takes. Keep those appointments, take your meds as directed. Don't turn to alcohol for answers. Have friends to call when you need an ear, and call the hotline for suicide prevention if you are at that point.

Never lose hope.

BRITTANY T.

I stuck half of a bobby pin into a candle flame and watched in awe as the plastic-coated tips melted off, until only the heated part of the metal remained. Touching it to my wrist in a deliberate circular shape filled me with a sense of purpose, a brief moment of reassurance in which I could believe that everything would be okay as long as I kept removing emotional agony by transforming it. I started puberty early, and soon after was raped by my neighbor at the age of eleven. I tried and failed to slit my wrists. To my parents, the rape did not matter—I downplayed it to them and to subsequent therapists because I could not cope with that pain on top of everything else. When I tell people I feel old at twenty-six, I still have trouble convincing them of my sincerity.

I pretended everything was fine while I starved myself to gain some semblance of control, and cut the inside of my thighs as a daily exercise in pain management. I took the charade further and began to make inappropriate jokes and comments so people could see how happy I was, until I could no longer keep up the ruse. Daily fights with my parents, numerous attempts by my father to strangle me, advanced anorexia, trouble getting along with peers in high school . . . I guess it all took a toll. I was finally put on a laundry list of medications over the course of six hospitalizations, and spoke with an endless parade of therapists.

Alcoholism runs in my family, and while I was not an alcoholic myself, I was told AA would be helpful to confront my addictive tendencies. I went, did the twelve steps in a way that was comfortable for me, and slowly began to realize a few things: 1) It's never wrong to stick up for yourself; 2) I am worth a great deal and have a lot to offer; 3) Being brutally honest might be tactless, but it's also one of my biggest expectations out of myself and others.

I started college and met the love of my life, my twin flame, the other half of my soul. I'd like to tell you that everything is groovy and my story ends happily with the two of us together facing the world, but my depression came back for a variety of reasons and I entertained a brief moment where I thought of ending my life. I want to feel better, but these things are easier said than done. I am still fighting to morph the intense pain I feel into understanding, into the ability to help others. I try to remember, above all, to love life and never let it go.

KIM K.

I was never simply okay. I was unhappy and cried all the time, or I was on top of the world. There was no middle ground. My brother always called me "high-strung." I did not have words like anxiety, depression, or mania to describe what I was experiencing. I turned to boys and thought that love and sex were the same. I made poor choices and had regrets. I was empty inside and I used alcohol and drugs to numb my feelings.

When one of my friends died in a car accident our junior year of high school, I didn't know how to cope with my grief. No one I had ever known had died. I sunk into what I know today was a very deep depression. I was in great pain and my thoughts were consumed by death. About a month later, I couldn't handle the pain anymore and I took a bottle of migraine medication with vodka. This was my first suicide attempt. I got scared as soon as I swallowed the pills and called a cousin for help. An ambulance came and took me to the emergency room. My parents and my family doctor were ignorant about mental illness, so they all just thought I was a rebellious teen who partied too much. No one knew what to do with me. I saw a couple of counselors, but I didn't trust them, so I wasn't able to tell them the truth. I'm not even sure I knew what the truth was—just that I continued to hurt.

I went through a series of suicide attempts and hospitalizations, and was finally diagnosed with bipolar I disorder. Along with taking my medication, I began to meet with a therapist weekly. My life slowly began to change. I wasn't up and down all the time, and my therapist helped me learn to live in the world. For the first time, I wasn't alone; I believed in myself and understood that I was not a failure because I have a mental illness.

Although I still find life challenging at times, I understand that problems have solutions. The symptoms of my illness have not completely disappeared and when I am under a lot of stress, they get worse. The difference today is that I know how to reach out for help. I do not have to stay stuck and live in misery. I have learned about my illness and myself, and I have developed coping skills. Life is good most days, and I am grateful to be alive.

TAMETRA T.

I thought that the loneliness would finally end. That all the pain would just go away. That I would just cry myself to sleep . . . and not wake up. There was no doubt in my mind that life on earth was not meant for me. Since the death of my grandparents, I'd felt abandoned and alone in a world I could not fight against by myself. It felt like a permanent nightmare.

I ingested a lethal dose of meds and cough syrup. Shutting off the lights and locking the door solidified the demise I was heading for. I woke up in pain, hoping death would come quicker. I called my sister for company. I kept the attempt to myself at first, but eventually

I started crying. In a couple of moments I knew I was going to pass out. So I told her the truth. She rushed me to the emergency room. The pain I felt could never amount to the pain I saw in the faces of all my family and friends when they found out what I did. They were confused as to why I could do something like this to myself. At that moment, I felt guilty and worthless. I was nothing but a burden. I knew I was better off dead and gone.

I was committed to a mental hospital, and it was the worst kind of nightmare. I sank into the deepest depressive hole imaginable. Seeing all those sick patients made *me* sick. I felt that I didn't belong there, and grew more depressed each day. All I had to hold on to was my teddy bear. I cried myself to sleep every night. There was no one to visit me. I could only talk on the phone for ten minutes a day. I missed school. I missed my sisters. Life could not have been any worse. It was at that moment that I really wished I was dead. I begged God to get me out of that mental ward, and promised Him I was going to work toward getting better and finding help for whatever problems I was facing.

Ultimately, my sister helped me understand that if I were dead and gone, life for my loved ones would never be the same. I was a vital piece in everyone's lives. I didn't understand because, at that moment, I truly believed no one cared about me. After that conversation, I realized that I was wrong. There's more to this life than the turmoil, the depression, and all the suffering put together.

ALLISON Q.

I had always tended to be a nervous person, so I didn't pay attention to warning signs that my common fears were becoming intensified and irrational. Days after my twenty-first birthday, I had a mental break that turned my life upside down. Suddenly, my anxiety and paranoia made it impossible for me to go out in public alone. Soon, I could no longer handle being home alone either. I constantly feared for my life. Within a few weeks, I could barely read or write. I was hospitalized five times, spending more than two months total admitted into the hospital. After many medication changes, they still were not sure about my diagnosis, but my doctors did find a medication that I responded to.

I tried going back to school, but I wasn't ready. I was so medicated that I would fall asleep during doctor's appointments, dinner, even during my sister's basketball games. I wasn't living my life.

Things all changed when my mom learned about psychiatric service dogs. After doing a lot of research, I found the dog who would change my life. Joey is the collie who helps me navigate the world. After months of training and socializing, he began to go everywhere with me.

With Joey, I could go places I hadn't been able to for years. I could sit with a friend and have coffee without having to examine and worry about every person who walked in the door. I was getting my confidence, independence, and vitality back. Joey made me feel protected and calm both in public and at home. He still has more training ahead of him, but the impact he has had on my life already is indescribable. I slowly began to transition off my strong antipsychotic, and now I feel healthier every day.

I want people to know that they should never, ever give up. Stay strong even when you feel like you have nothing left; things will always work out eventually. Before recovery, I wasn't a believer in fate, but now I see it all around me, every day.

K.T.

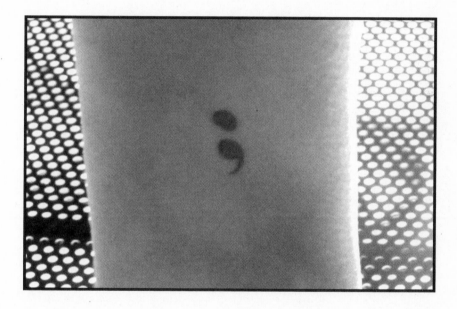

I've always known how to play the game. I knew when and how to appear, exactly what to say and what not to say. I perfected the art of surviving amid a childhood of severe trauma.

Sexually abused from infancy until my preteen years by those closest to me, I was robbed of my innocence and left forever marked. Like most victims of sexual abuse, I never told a single soul, heeding my father's threats as he wrapped his hands around my small throat: "If you tell anyone, I will wring your neck."

I learned how to be silent. I learned how to keep secrets. I learned to survive.

My first suicide attempt was at eight years old; my last would be thirty years later. The years in between consisted of hiding the pain; I started cutting to manage my emotions and the secrets buried deep inside of me. On the outside I appeared strong, confident, and equipped to handle all life threw my way. I hid who I was from the world and from myself.

One night, I found myself on my knees sobbing uncontrollably, a butcher knife pressed to my wrist. I was begging, pleading, in pain-fueled desperation, screaming out to God that I would do anything if He'd only take the pain away. I had reached the point where the pain was so unbearable, ending my life seemed like a reasonable choice.

As I watched the knife, red began to drip down my arm. Looking up at the ceiling, I heard myself say, "I surrender!" The knife fell to the floor and clarity entered my foggy mind. I knew I needed help.

In the months that followed, my therapist revealed his findings to me: borderline personality disorder, dissociative identity disorder, complex post-traumatic stress disorder, delusional tendencies with dissociative fugue. Making the choice to first accept my diagnosis and then commit to working through the trauma of my childhood was the hardest thing I have done. Fear of rejection by my close friends, my siblings, and society haunted me, and it caused increased panic attacks.

After diligently working through my past, being proactive in managing my mental health, forgiving my abusers, using tools to cope with the day-to-day while living with mental illness, learning to forgive myself, and allowing myself to be loved, I am happy and feel whole. Life is enjoyable at last.

AARON C.

Nobody could understand how a kid like me who was always happy, smiling, and telling jokes could suddenly be afraid of everything and depressed about "simple" things. My mom decided to take me to a psychologist and, after some treatment, the psychologist thought it'd be a better idea for me to see a psychiatrist, who started giving me antidepressants.

Things didn't change much and I continued having suicidal thoughts. I went from medicine to medicine, feeling like I was a guinea pig for the doctor. I started going out more, but only so I could have an excuse to drink. It was long-term suicide; the drinks kept coming and the mood swings got bigger and bigger until I started seeing other doctors, who all agreed that I didn't have depression, but bipolar II disorder.

My family supported me, but somehow didn't give my disorder as much attention as they would have given any other disease. I saw many doctors, but I kept bouncing from one to another. This was because they all said I should be in a mental hospital, and my parents weren't okay with that idea. This is where the stigma started to kick me hard. I couldn't find a way out without putting an end to my own life.

I remember the day when I made my first suicide attempt; I was at my brother's house, feeling at peace with myself. I had decided my job in this life was done, so after a talk with my brother, I took a bottle of rum and some anxiolytics I had hidden in my backpack. I swallowed the pills with almost half the bottle of rum, then waited for everything to kick in. I woke up in a hospital with some tubes inside my nose and the image of my brother crying.

After that attempt, my parents watched me closer, but still refused to put me in a mental hospital. I kept dealing by using alcohol, and soon drugs. I was trying to call death to meet me. I took dangerous roads, trying to find a feeling that would kill the one already inside of me. So one day, out of the blue, I took my car and drove while drinking a bottle of whiskey. While I was out, some guy started pushing me for no reason. He then took a small baseball bat and hit me with it . . . I don't remember much, but some pieces in my memory tell me that I woke up in the middle of some street, hurt, with my face disfigured. I looked like a monster.

I had some brain damage and stayed in the hospital for a week and a half. My senses of smell and taste don't work the way they used to, and since the injury, I am more aggressive. I also started hallucinating.

I found information about a ten-K race on the internet. To be honest, I still don't know why I chose to do it. Maybe it was the echo of my parents and ex-girlfriend saying I was so unstable, I couldn't finish anything. It wasn't a big deal, but I wanted to show them that I could finish a race, so I prepared, ran the race, and completed it.

I noticed while preparing for that race that running kept me motivated and away from alcohol. I followed plans to finish other races, but in one of my trainings I tore a ligament in my knee. I had surgery, an implant, and terrible news: after my knee rehab I could no longer run long-distance races anymore, only short ones . . . so my demons came back.

A year later, I got tired of it all. I was tired of not being able to run and of not being able to feel stable, so I began to run again. I thought if I could handle inner pain, physical pain wouldn't be anything. I was harming my body whether I chose to drink myself to death or run on my knee, so I decided I would rather run.

I can say now that alcohol isn't an issue for me. I've run six marathons, including an ultramarathon, and tons of half marathons, without having to visit the doctor again. My knee is fine, and I'm better. I still struggle with hallucinations, a bad temper, and mood swings, but now I have a blessing that God gave me: running.

RACHEL B.

Self-harming had become so much a part of me by high school that my friends had all but accepted it and learned to ignore it. My family were still, for the most part, unaware, as I hid my shame carefully to preserve their feelings.

Then came the boy.

I loved to pretend he cared; I spent an entire year forming an image of him in my head that, essentially, did not exist. Whenever he found out I had hurt myself, he showed absolutely zero concern, and when I went a week or so without, he would give me a "congratulations" full of contempt. Looking back, it was ignorant and patronizing, but I got into my head the wonderful idea that this person was more proud of me when I was clean than ashamed when I wasn't. We made a promise that for Lent I would give up my addiction if he gave up his. Soon I found out he had secretly not kept his side of the deal at all, and it was then I realized that it is not anyone else's job to be proud of me—it's mine. One night, entirely alone, scared, and facing the terrible truth that this was my job and no one else's, I dug my knuckles into the carpet until they bled one final time. Then I started anew.

The time between then and now has been a struggle. One relapse, two years of university, and an irresponsibly spontaneous trip to Thailand to try to sort myself out later, I have learned a very important thing: the most essential part of anyone's story is the moment when you start to comprehend that your most trusted counselor, doctor, and friend is the person looking straight back at you in the mirror. This isn't nearly as depressing as it sounds.

I have an incredible network of friends and family, a sister who has saved my life more times than I appreciate, and a boyfriend who showed me how I deserve to be treated in a relationship. But I never would have formed healthy relationships with these amazing people until I developed a comfortable and stable sense of self. Shame is a useless emotion that comes to us most often in retrospect. But if I had let that shame define me, I would still be with someone who lured me into false pacts and a destructive, fake, manipulative relationship. Accepting yourself is a responsibility that falls to you and you alone.

ULRIKE P.

As a child, I felt sick a lot—usually in the evenings, or in the morning on my way to school. One night, I was feeling sick and lying in bed. I accidentally bumped my head against the bed frame and it hurt so badly that I did not feel sick anymore.

That's when I learned you can transform pain with other pain.

After that, I started using my fingernail to press into my wrist when I felt sick. This hurt and relaxed me at the same time. I always carried this self-harm with me over the next few years, but I never really cared about it. Eventually, I got so sick that I couldn't eat properly anymore. A range of doctors couldn't find any physical cause for my symptoms. My social life was nonexistent; I stayed home most of the time.

I started therapy. I discovered I was carrying a whole lot of insecurity, black-and-white thinking, panic, fear of loss, and problems with social bonds. I was convinced that the people I loved would be better off without me. That's about when I realized that self-harm could not only transfer physical pain, but also mental pain.

Whenever my low self-esteem kicked in and I was feeling inadequate, I would hurt myself. I started with the fingernail and ended up with a knife. I just did not know any other way to handle the emotional conflict within me.

I switched therapists and was diagnosed with borderline personality disorder. Cognitive behavioral therapy has helped me learn to calm down, and I've also learned to love and respect myself. That's still hard sometimes, but I am on my way.

RACHEL B.

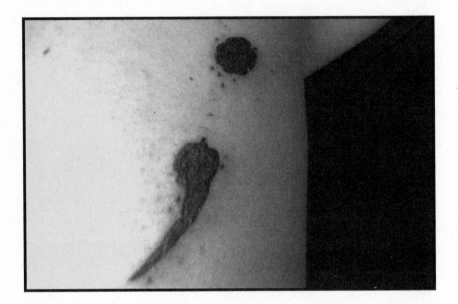

I lost everything, including my marriage and my family. I tried to carry on, but I wasn't coping. I'm ashamed to admit I tried overdosing. Getting the help I needed meant losing my job, but in hindsight, taking time away to heal was the best thing ever. A year later, I'm still fighting, but I'm stronger than I was before.

ROBYN R.

Looking back, I see why I picked food for my comfort. I could eat to feel happy and good. I also believed that if I got bigger, maybe my abuser wouldn't touch me again. It didn't seem to make a difference. When I got into high school, the family member was no longer around to abuse me anymore, but I became bulimic—binging to feel better, then purging to get rid of the mess I put into my body. I told myself I wouldn't be able to find someone to love me if I stayed big and ugly. I had to become pretty in order to have someone love me for who I really wanted to be. I got attention, but the attention that was given to me was a facade.

The first boy I thought loved me for me became my high school sweetheart. I grabbed onto the attention because this someone was giving me love—or so I thought. The relationship ended after he became extremely controlling, cheated on me, and was jealous of any time I spent apart from him. I became depressed, had anxiety and panic attacks, and developed behavior problems. Suicidal thoughts came to mind, but I couldn't go through with it because I didn't want to cause pain to anyone else. I knew what it was like to hurt and live with pain.

Through all of this chaos, I have been diagnosed with clinical depression with a behavioral disorder. I take medication to help my cycles be more stable and to help with the anxiety. My life cycles through highs and lows, but my heart keeps beating. I love my life, and myself, enough to carry on.

BETTY L.

Growing up, I didn't know what was wrong with me. I cried so easily and felt different; I never seemed to fit in, like there was a hole in me and something was missing. I wanted real friends, but it rarely happened. I was lucky because I didn't turn to drugs, alcohol, or hurting myself, but I did turn to retail therapy. I had some really dark times, such that I don't remember them, but others do. I was told to "suck it up" and "get over" myself—you know the words. I thought many times that my family would be happier if I didn't exist, but could never end my story.

I wasn't diagnosed with depression until later in life, and then I began the game of trying to find which meds would work the best. The chosen medications helped and my world seemed better. I felt better, happy, joyful, and full of promise. I still battled the demons occasionally, but knew what to look for so it was easier to realize what was happening.

Then I fell backward from a truck's tailgate, straight back from eight feet high, onto a concrete garage floor. I suffered a pretty intense concussion that started the darkest period in my life I'd ever known. The fall and hitting my head spiraled me down into worse thoughts than I'd ever experienced. There were voices telling me I was worthless and that everyone would be better off without me. They almost convinced me to wrap my car around a telephone pole or tree.

I still have depression. It's not something that goes away or "has a cure." You don't just "get over it," but a year later, I'm in a place I never thought I'd be in: a place of peace, contentment, joy, and happiness.

MICHELLE A.

I had been in a committed relationship with depression my entire life. Not out of choice, but because I knew I would never be able to leave. I was isolated in my misery, hiding behind a tattooed smile. And on the days I could no longer do that, I locked myself away where I would not be able to subject anyone else to my pain.

The day of my diagnosis was the beginning of my road to healing.

I have thrown myself into research and continue to learn about how to manage my life successfully—and sometimes happily—around my partner, depression (who occasionally has a temper tantrum of mania). I have learned that bipolar disorder brings a lot of unexpected gifts and road maps to direct me to where I'm hurting and need help. I am dedicated to my healing and transformation, go to regular therapy, and stick religiously to my medication.

I can now reach out for help when I feel weak, and on days when I'm strong—and even when I'm not—I stretch out my own hand to help others climbing out of the same abyss. It isn't easy, but it's also not hopeless. I choose to believe my life has the potential for a very happy ending.

REMMELT M.

One day I decided I no longer wanted to let depression consume me; I wanted to win, and the only way out was through suicide. My brain told me it would be easy to just die; nobody would miss me. Multiple times, I stood at the train tracks waiting to get the guts to step forward and end my pain once and for all.

The day arrived: the day I should die. I wrote my family and the few friends I had farewell letters and hopped on my bike to return to the train tracks.

My uncle happened to see me and my tears. He almost pulled me off my bike, telling me we had to talk. He shared his own story about his depression and suicide attempts. I realized there were still people who loved me, still beautiful things to live for.

Slowly but surely, I crawled out from under the darkness and back into the light. Yes, there are still moments of darkness—some longer than others—but I will always come back out into the light!

ANDREA L.

I have always put on a brave face and done what people expected me to do, but I usually feel like an imposter. Feelings of inadequacy are constantly floating around in my thoughts. *I'm not good enough. I'm not special. I'm not intelligent. I'll never amount to anything.* I once thought about suicide, and how ending my life would mean I wouldn't have the worry hanging over my head anymore, wouldn't experience those lost feelings that subside to a constant numbness.

Ultimately, I knew suicide wasn't an option because I could not bear to burden my family with that much pain. You see, I am the "strong one," the one my family comes to when there's a problem. I am the rock. What would happen to them if I was not here?

One afternoon when I was at home, I broke down. I hadn't been able to get myself to do anything that day; life was too much. I collapsed on the floor in tears, yet nothing had happened to made me cry. I called my mom, who rushed over and ended up holding me until I could calm down. She convinced me to schedule an appointment with my doctor. A few days later, I went to that appointment and asked my doctor to run tests to rule out any possible medical issues that could be causing my symptoms. The results came in: I was in great physical health. He diagnosed me with depression. We spoke about antidepressants and chose one together. We decided on a treatment plan, and then he sent me on my way. I got in my car and the totality of the past year, plus the diagnosis, hit me and I cried.

I wanted my semicolon tattoo to be in a watercolor style, because mental health is not perfect; it is a messy, constant battle and I wanted that reflected in my tattoo. The black represents my depression, and the colors represent the hope that comes with winning the battle at the end of every day.

ANNIE B.

I was ten years old when I was sexually abused by my babysitter. Even though my parents suspected, it went on for months. For a long time I kept everything a secret because I'd made a deal with my babysitter to spare my siblings in exchange for me. I blamed myself for all of it and couldn't consider myself a victim because I'd helped write the rules: me for them. There was nobody to protect me. I was utterly alone.

When the truth came out that I had been raped, the silence was crippling. I was expected to "get over it." Apathy, silence, victim shaming—I saw it all.

That feels like a lifetime ago now: I fell in love, got married, moved to a new country where I found myself surrounded by people who care about me, scars and all. Through their love and kindness I sought help, and it was then that I found out I had PTSD. So much fell into place from knowing I wasn't "just crazy" and it wasn't "just me." That's when the real healing began.

When the darkness comes, and it does (though not nearly as often), I remember that there is light and hope, and people out there I can talk to. I will always keep fighting. I'm not alone anymore. It has taken a lot to get this far. Owning my story has given me a courage I didn't know I possessed. And it has opened up so many doors and torn down so many walls that I didn't know were there. It's empowering. Terrifying at times, too. But I'm braver than I give myself credit for. I've come so far, and there's so much more still to do.

DAWN S.

My mom and I didn't realize that my phobia of ordering food at restaurants or my extreme fear of driving were by-products of anxiety. Growing up, I just avoided those situations and tried to deal. Twenty years later, I'm just now starting to understand what depression and anxiety do to me and the people in my life—but it took a lot to get to this point.

My husband had been dealing with addiction for a couple years, and as our relationship became more and more toxic, my mental health steadily declined, too. As he continued to use, I felt more and more hopeless—not only as a wife but as a person. I couldn't talk about my situation with my friends and family because, to them, it was so easy: just leave my husband and let him deal with his own issues. This is easier said than done. I had begun to self-harm in an effort to control something in my life, since my husband's addiction was beyond my control. I was afraid for both of us.

So there I was, at two in the morning, sitting on my couch with all these sleeping pills in my hand. (My husband was suffering from withdrawal in the bedroom, but he was finally asleep for a few precious minutes.) I decided I would hurt too many people taking the easy way out. I didn't do it; I needed to reach out for help. It made me feel selfish, like I was abandoning my husband, but I needed to do something—and quickly.

I left the house later that morning and attempted to kiss my husband good-bye. I was pretending to leave for work, though I had texted my mom to take me to the hospital. It was so hard to leave, but I did. I was scared beyond measure. I couldn't wait to get checked into the behavioral health hospital so they could take my phone and I could have an excuse for not texting him or calling him back. It felt like it took forever, but once I was there, it was like a weight was lifted off my shoulders.

I was in the hospital for five days. I just worked on myself and on getting well. My husband came to see me a couple of days into my stay, once I finally reached out to him. He was angry because he felt like I'd abandoned him while he was still in the grip of withdrawal. But now that some time has passed, he understands that I did what I needed to do. That stay at the hospital was the best thing I could have done for myself.

It's now been a year and I am in a much better frame of mind. My husband is a year clean and is properly medicated for his bipolar disorder. I have been going to group therapy ever since treatment and it has been amazing. I love sharing my story and talking about the lowest point in my life, because I want to help others who are suffering like I was.

You are not alone, and sharing your story and helping others is the best way to continue to do well and feel better.

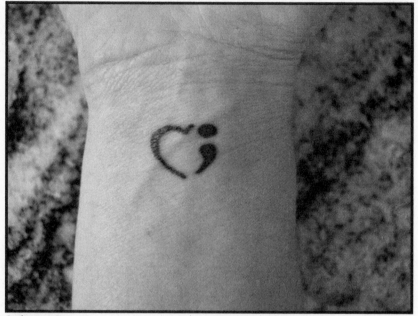

Catherine C.

Dana C.

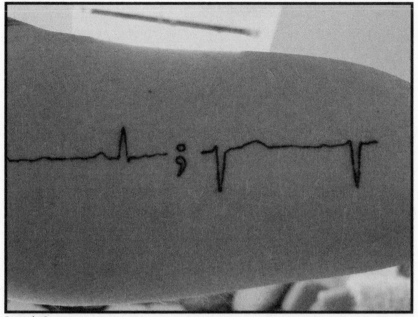

Daniela S.

Jennifer L.

JORDAN M.

Anxiety is more than just stress. It is staying still because you are unable to move. It is rocking back and forth, not being able to speak at all, uncontrollable shaking, crying so much you can't breathe. It's feeling like your head can't take any more thoughts, movements, or gestures because it will explode. It's being frozen in time but in a very dangerous situation you can't escape.

Two things help me pass through dark times: writing and dancing. When I write, it creates another world in paper and ink, a place I can go to express what I can't always say out loud. With dance, there is so much I can feel about myself when I start to point and flex my feet. Lyrical dancing is another reality, another world to me. When I start to move, I can let everything go—all the worries, the anxiety, the sadness. It all disappears for a while. It's a feeling I want to keep forever, until nothing else exists—like I'm sleeping on a cloud.

My anxiety and depression have helped me discover another part of myself. I am proud to have made it this far and plan to continue my journey.

JAIRO M.

I was sitting in sophomore English doing group work when, out of nowhere, I began crying and shaking like a nervous wreck. I tried to shrug it off at first, but soon my breathing was fast and heavy. Within seconds, I lost all feeling in my body; I vividly remember curling into a ball right at my desk. This was my first panic attack.

But the panic attack itself wasn't the problem.

The problem that still haunts me today was that when I finally calmed down, I saw people openly laughing at me. Others were desperately trying to hold back their laughter. I don't blame those who just stood watching—I wouldn't have known what to do either—but how people could laugh at the situation is something I will never comprehend. All the anxiety came rushing back and I was at the point of fainting, but I remained conscious, numb, and drowned in tears, all while being mercilessly ridiculed. I was escorted out of the classroom in a wheelchair, not knowing that this was the start of my journey with mental illnesses.

Later on that day, I had my second panic attack. The day after, my third. Then my fourth, and fifth, and sixth, and every day I started to have at least one attack. I was exhibiting the critical symptoms of anxiety disorders, depression, and post-traumatic stress disorder. Soon my friends started to abandon me, saying that I was "infested with problems" and that they didn't want to deal with me anymore. After a couple of months, it was pretty much just me, with the exception of some loyal friends who stuck by my side.

I felt isolated, afraid of people and their judgment. I started developing the early signs of schizophrenia: I would see figures (especially shadows), hear voices, and fear for my life. I remember one day sitting in my chemistry class and hearing voices in my head tell me, "Kill yourself. Just kill yourself." At that moment, my "what would happen if" suicidal thoughts morphed into drastically outlined plans of how I was going to commit suicide. I remember holding a rope in my hand and putting it around my neck for what felt like hours before I finally put it down and shouted, "I just can't!"

My body was worn down to the last tear I could produce. Fatigue hit me every day like a train, leaving me unable to even speak properly. Suicide was the only action on my mind at this point, but my body lacked the energy it required to pick up a knife, or a rope, or even a gun. I don't know how I survived those darkest weeks, but one day soon after . . . the attacks stopped. The anxiety remained, but never enough for me to have an attack. The schizophrenic thoughts remained, but I no longer feared the shadows and voices I would encounter. For once in almost two years, I felt the confidence I needed to hold my head high and create peace with my suicidal thoughts. This attack-free lifestyle would last for about two years before I ran into problems again.

Spring quarter of my first year of college, I finally had another attack. This was by far one of the scariest attacks I've ever had because it assured me that even if I was completely at peace for some time, there was still a possibility of returning to ground zero with my disorders.

It has now been a year since my attacks regressed and I am still fighting every single day. Unlike before, I don't have four attacks a day but rather one a month—proof positive that life will get better even when it seems dire.

I am a person who survived the feeling of being drowned and burned alive at the same time, every day, for nearly five years. I will wear my body's scars proudly. I will wave my muscle spasms, tears, gray hairs, and every single last gasp of breath as a flag in tribute to my struggle. I am doing everything I can to make sure I love myself and will not quit on myself. I will continue my fight against my disorders and even if the war may never be over, I will win every battle with a smile, one deep breath at a time.

MARIANNE D.

In Memoriam

I haven't seen you in years. You were supposed to come back.

In an ideal world, you would have come back. You would have come back, picked up your medications, and taken them religiously, as if your life depended on it.

Because it did.

Today, you stopped me in my tracks in the hallway. Two years later.

Your face, with all the harsh angles. Your eyes, so full of defeat.

You gave up. You gave up.

I do not want to look you in the eyes. But I force myself to. I tell myself to keep my poker face. Complete the task.

But you are not a task. You are a human being. A person. With a heartbeat. And a soul that is burdened.

You grieved your father's death, and you could not deal. You did not know how to deal. You just wanted to run away. It was easier. This white powdered best friend helped you, more than anyone else did. But it's toxic. And it landed you in jail. The cycle continues.

Here you are with me. In pain. With a fever. Helpless. You ask me if you can go home. Though I calmly tell you "soon," it will not be soon. You lean on my desk. And you wait.

One phone call.

Two phone calls.

Three.

One application.

Another phone call.

You gave me your trust. To do things on your behalf.

I do not want the power to choose which hospice you should go to.

But you gave up.

Even after you leave, because you could no longer sit still from your pain, my heart aches for you. And I sit in dread and in tears. Knowing that your story will soon end, because you will not fight.

You send me an email. Full of gratitude. And what is this? Is it a shimmer of hope? Is it a hope for life? Or hope for death? I cannot tell.

But I tell you what's next, logistically.

And then, unexpectedly, I plead.

I plead for you to fight.

I plead for you to fight, if not for yourself, then for your mother, who lost her husband and may lose her son.

I tell you about the living miracles I have seen walking through these halls. Miracles because of the ounce of hope they have.

It was the ounce that mattered.

If it were up to me, I would have enough hope for you. I would have enough fight for you. But it doesn't work that way.

I sit. And I wait. For what happens next.

SONYA S.

My dad was an alcoholic. He had a mean temperament when he was sober, but it became much worse when he drank. He never physically abused any of us kids, but he did hit our mom. Emotionally, he scarred me. I can still hear the things he would say to me.

When depression hit during my college years, it hit hard. I found myself in my closet crying uncontrollably, feeling so hopeless. What was my purpose? My sister convinced me to talk to someone. I began to see a psychiatrist, who has helped me so much. I am not a fan of taking medication, but it is what keeps me going.

Just as I was starting to cope with my depression, I received a phone call that completely changed me forever. *"Your dad has shot himself."* The news brought me to my knees. Granted, I did not have a close relationship with my dad, but that news sent me into a tailspin. I didn't understand how he could do that, to us, to our mom.

I was eventually able to understand why my dad did what he felt he had to do. He was a very prideful man who always said he would never be a burden to anyone. I guess he saw no way out. I knew I could not do that to my loved ones. I cried out to God, who is merciful, gracious, powerful, almighty, forgiving, and loving. He has been my strength. Do I still have tough days? Sure I do, but I know that I have the hope of eternal life, and that helps me to deal with my depression.

> *So do not fear, for I am with you; do not be dismayed, for I am our God. I will strengthen you and help you; I will uphold you with my righteous right hand.*
>
> *—Isaiah 41:10*

JENNIFER B.

While most of my friends were looking forward to going off to university and starting exciting new chapters in their lives, I was working two jobs, taking twenty-two hours of course credits, and caring for ailing parents. Soon my own health started to fail me. Everything made me vomit. I couldn't hold down food or water. Standing for too long made me feel faint. Walking to classes took me twice as long as it once had. I feared the worst; I thought I might have lung cancer, like my mother. Three times I was taken to the ER only to be sent home with "the flu," but this went on for months.

My best friend abandoned me, and many of my other friends just stopped inviting me to functions after a while. They assumed I was dead to the world. Stressed out, sick, and isolated, I fought through the motions of routine. Then one of my biggest motivators was gone: my dad passed away at home while I was at the hospital. I felt miserable mentally and physically. Just empty and blank. I was in a state of shock. This was not my dream of life after high school. I was in a nightmare that I couldn't wake up from.

In the end, my dad's memories kept me going. My whole life, he'd used song lyrics to address problems. Country, rock-and-roll, Disney, Broadway—it didn't matter. There was a song for every issue. One song he used to sing often was "You'll Never Walk Alone." The day after he died, it was storming, and I sat outside in the rain. Crying and sopping wet, I watched the storm disperse as the sun's rays began to break through the dark clouds. Dad's favorite song played back in my mind: "At the end of the storm, there's a golden sky." The aftermath of the storm I was going through would be beautiful—I just had to make it through.

Ultimately, Mother lost a lung and I lost a gallbladder. I had been suffering from a bad case of gallstones. Since I was diagnosed and had surgery, my health has gotten much better. I started running regularly and trained for my first half marathon. During a literal storm, I met my fiancé, Charles. His smile brightened the gloom of that dismal day. I still miss my dad. He will not be able to walk me down the aisle at my wedding, but he will always be with me.

BINDI S.

I was six when my sister and her boyfriend took their lives. For the next seven years, I was in therapy once a week. At seventeen, I was trapped in a violent relationship. I was nothing. Good for nothing. Nobody. There were times I just wished he'd choke me that little bit harder. Everything was wrong with me and I was sadder than I'd ever been before. I drank too much. I took too many pills. I'd hold my breath, hoping that his tight grip on my throat would finish the job. But it didn't. It never did.

Eventually, I escaped. I continued with my life as I knew it, feeling worthless, inadequate, and sad. On the outside, I was confident and happy. On the inside, I was seething with self-loathing. The extrovert everyone thought they knew had secrets—secrets that happy people just don't understand.

Later, I met the man of my dreams. So caring, so loving, and so into me. Things started to look brighter. But they weren't. Pills and liquor. Cutting. Why wouldn't I die? Why was it so hard to end my life? More secrets. Secrets I kept from someone who loved me, cared about me. I couldn't breathe, couldn't stop crying. Even though I had a wonderful man in my life, I had never felt so alone.

I decided to go back to therapy. I was diagnosed with depression, anxiety, panic attacks, and PTSD. As if being depressed wasn't enough, I was living with quite the cocktail of sordid emotions. Twice a week I'd see my therapist. Sometimes it felt good to talk to her. Sometimes we just sat there in silence for an hour. Sometimes I wanted to punch her in the throat.

My therapist taught me how to take control of my anxiety. She taught me how to breathe. Just breathe. That overwhelming feeling that hits you like a cannonball to the gut? I can breathe through that now. When I feel a panic attack getting ready to strike, I sing. I sing and I breathe. Most times I can get through it without wanting to curl up into a ball and die.

Most of my past therapy sessions are a blur to me now. I've learned to look forward. I've learned to talk to those who are trying to help me instead of pushing them away. I'm recovering, but it's a slow process. Do I sometimes feel like it's not worth the effort? Yes, but I'm growing. I'm taking each day as it comes. I will not be defeated.

KAYLA T.

One day in eighth grade, my class had to fill out a sexual abuse survey. I got to the first question, began to sob uncontrollably, and told my teacher I could not fill out the survey. I bolted out of the classroom, ran to the nurse, and told her about the abuse I had been experiencing. Social services got involved; I was interviewed by a detective at our local police department. They declared me a victim of abuse at the hands of my own father.

I felt like no one cared about me. I felt like if I were to die, no one would notice. I was lost. I had already been self-harming for a while, but around this time, it became apparent I had serious problems with self-injury and eating disorders, and I was even struggling with my own existence. Anxiety and depression were stealing the best of me. My friends and teachers were concerned for me, but I did not want help, so it was nearly impossible for me to change my ways. Much later, after I realized I needed help and sought counseling, I was still not satisfied with life and just wanted to be free from all the pain.

Everything changed when I met the boy who would become the man I'll be marrying next year. I hadn't been looking for a relationship, but here was this guy who I thought was so adorable, who I knew immediately would never hurt me. I started going to church with him and his family, and soon I was transformed from someone who hated God into someone who loves Him unconditionally.

I still have noticeable scars on my body from self-harm, but they are just reminders of what I have been through. Each one tells a story, and I know God has been with me every step of the way.

DEREK R.

In the sixth or seventh grade, I relied on music to get me through the difficult fits of anxiety, when it would feel like every breath was a struggle and there was an elephant standing on my chest.

This was when I began to self-harm. I would cut my arms and legs to feel something. The bits of blood reminded me that I was alive and that inside the empty shell I walked around in day to day was a life—even though I didn't know quite how to experience it. No matter how hard I tried, I wasn't a piece that could force itself to fit in this puzzle called life. Luckily, in these moments of contemplating whether I should be here, or if I should end my story before it really started, I found renewed faith through a Psalm. I read Psalm 69:4 and had a fresh sense of hope that I was meant for more, and that I could restore the shambles my young life had become.

By high school, I was handling my depression and anxiety fits with therapy and medication. I'd gotten to a point where I'd found some balance in my life, even in my social life. Then tragedy struck: one morning during my freshman year, I woke to the news that my father had committed suicide. My parents had been going through a separation and things were very difficult and awkward at home. All the emotions had come to a head, and I guess he saw no other way out. I had no idea that my father had fought the same kind of mental demons I had, some to an even greater extent.

Life stopped . . . everything decayed. This wonderful hope in my life that had been gaining so much momentum crashed, along with the relationships I had with my family. I watched as my mother, my biggest fan and hero, crumpled to her knees in emotional agony. My brother was left broken; he and my father had been very close, leaving him, essentially, without his best friend. We struggled to make ends meet. I was illegally driving to go work in a restaurant from open to close all summer long. I was so focused on helping my family that I didn't have time to fall apart.

By the time I went to college, fell in love, got married, got a job, and basically did all the things I'd wanted to do since I was sixteen, I had accepted that while my armor didn't shine anymore, it could withstand the battle. Four years into the marriage, tragedy struck me again: she had fallen out of love. My heart was completely and utterly torn out. Since the passing of my father, I had struggled a great deal with feeling good enough. Had I not been good enough for him to stay? Had I not been good enough for him to say good-bye? What had I done wrong?

It's been almost three years since the divorce was finalized. The peaks and valleys in those years have been deeper than oceans and higher than mountaintops. But I'm still breathing.

If there's one thing I've learned through my trials, it is that there's always a silver lining, even if you're unable to see it. As a man of Christian faith, I know that trials and tribulations are meant to build me up and make me better, even if I can't find a particle of reasoning behind it. It's okay . . . it's okay because you are wonderful; every special piece of you was designed for amazing things. There will be days when you're sad, and that's okay, too, because without that sadness you can't appreciate the deserved happiness that will come your way. There is so much love around us if you'll look through the smoke; somewhere, someone is struggling through the same things you are, and they love you. They don't know you, but they love every little thing about you.

You deserve wonderful things.

ERIC P.

On a night I will never forget, I decided that my life wasn't worth living anymore. I had a plan to take my life after I finished my shift at work that night. I would go home to my apartment and leave this world.

When the hour arrived for me to go home, I found myself driving to the hospital instead. I checked myself into the hospital and stayed there for roughly a week. That week was the greatest week of my life. It was then that I realized I wasn't alone in this battle and there were people who could help me with this fight. I met some truly amazing people there who saved me in more ways than I ever could have imagined. They taught me ways to cope with my anxiety and not let it build within me. They taught me that life is precious and that I wasn't alone.

I started to find peace with myself and started to take care of myself in multiple ways. I was able to open up to my family and friends and finally realize how big of a support system I truly had.

I will not lie and say that every day is a walk in the park. I still have those dark days, but I am learning to cope with them in healthy ways. I want every single person out there to know that you are not alone in this. You are stronger that you think, I promise you that.

CASSIDY F.

I read this quote a while back that said: "You own everything that happened to you. Tell your stories. If people wanted you to write warmly about them, they should've behaved better." That alone soothes some of the great amount of anxiety I get from talking about my life. Both my parents struggled with alcohol and drug addictions, which means I really grew up in a war zone. Fighting and screaming every night, slamming cabinets and doors that sounded like gunshots, windows and doors being kicked in . . . every single night. Then I would wake up and go to school like nothing had happened. My parents stressed how important it was to keep quiet about what goes on behind closed doors, but eventually, Child Protective Services separated my siblings and me from each other and our parents. I went into foster care with the highest of expectations. Finally, I would have a loving, normal family. But my foster family made me feel like everything was my fault. They reduced me to nothing. They became the voices in my head.

At last, I moved into a residence hall at a local university: I was free. This newfound freedom ignited a fire that I'd buried deep inside of me. All of the tragedies I had been put through were starting to surface. I would have flashbacks and nightmares. I discovered what lucid dreaming was. I hated being touched; loud banging noises made me flinch and triggered flashbacks to slamming cabinets and doors. I had my first panic attack during this time. It all became too much, and the suicidal thoughts that had been in the background of my mind were now in full bloom. I would spend every sleepless night planning my funeral like it was a wedding. A guest list, the flowers, would it be in a church or outside?

At that point, I had evolved from pinching and popping myself to cutting on my thigh. Looking back, it's all a little hazy, like I was a zombie. I would go into a state of dreamless daydreaming all day, every day. I couldn't kill myself because I didn't want to hurt my sister or my mom, but I thought if they knew how miserable I was, they would understand.

One summer, I stayed with my best friend. She knew how depressed I was, but that summer she got to see it, too. Some days I wouldn't even get out of bed. She was worried and told her mom. They both begged me to get help. I only agreed because of the massive amount of guilt I felt in bringing such darkness into her home. I went to a clinic, where I was taken in through crisis and immediately enrolled into their services. Recovery wouldn't come quickly, but it had begun.

Talking about my self-harm and putting my suicidal thoughts into words is the scariest thing I have ever done. For nineteen years, I told myself I shouldn't hurt because I could've had it worse. I had also been taught to keep everything inside. So opening up was hard, but I did it. I did it. I faced my worst nightmare and it has been the most rewarding thing. My counselor is heaven-sent. She has taken me under her wing and she displays a parental love I have never experienced. I feel safe with her. Safe from everything, including myself.

I look back to last year and see a whole lot of darkness. But now I have so much light in my life. I am loved by many and I am loved by myself. I haven't self-harmed in a year and I no longer plan my own funeral. Instead, I plan for my future; I am pursuing a degree in business and intend to obtain a master's in psychology and counseling. I want to be the light in other people's darkness for the rest of my life.

I just want to sign off by saying THERE IS HOPE FOR YOU. This is coming from a person who was convinced for years that there was no hope. I've seen it personally. I've lived it. Keep going.

ADELE F.

When the shroud of depression starts to envelop me, it is stealthy. First it takes away my easy smiles and laughter. It shortens my fuse, so I may be that little bit harder on my children or more easily provoked. I do not feel the shroud across my shoulders, but it is there.

Then the shroud is at my knees and I know. By the time I realize I am no longer well, I refuse to take action. My perceptions of situations are skewed and influenced by the disease now. I am anxious about many things as my mind races to make sure I keep going. Life stress is no longer something I can cope with because I am consumed with getting through work, social activities, and family life.

Disturbing moments happen where I consider self-harm or suicide and these moments become more frequent. I am exhausted, compelled to sleep at any opportunity. Sleep is the time when my mind stops. It is the only real relaxation.

Then one day the shroud is dragging on the floor and I can no longer walk. I stumble and can't move forward. I didn't see it coming so devastatingly quickly; some saw it coming and others didn't notice.

For twelve months my psychiatrist has been asking if I could take a break from what I was doing; make no big decisions and just take care. I don't heed his advice and I break.

Surrendering to the shroud is both liberating and terrifying. Help is finally here, but at what cost? What has become of my life? I collapse into the safety of my home and try to accept how unwell I am. I try to push away the feelings of guilt and by doing so add more guilt. Talking is hard, moving is hard, leaving the house borders on impossible. I am now a shell merely existing. I scare myself with dark thoughts of what value I am to my family and friends.

A switch is flicked in my brain one day. The right combination of medications, the time it's taken for them to work, the weeks of nearly complete rest, and the love and support from my family and friends are starting to work. It is obvious to me there has been a change. Then all of a sudden the shroud is back up to my waist. Just like that. I talk to my psychiatrist about how quickly this seems to occur and he shares that many people have similar experiences.

I walk outside and, for the first time since I stumbled, I can feel the air gently brushing against my skin. I hear better and I see better. My mind is no longer a constant fog. Both my mind and my environment seem clearer. I can laugh and smile. I can look forward to comfortable time with friends. Am I cured? No, I don't believe this illness has a cure. Am I all better for now? No, this is a critical time to ensure I don't let the shroud slip. I can do it, I can make sure the shroud doesn't slip. It takes work and energy.

This is where the story ends for me this time. The shroud will continue to lift and I will go back to living instead of merely existing. I will try to avoid provoking symptoms of my chronic illness. Just as a diabetic medicates and manages their health, I will need to do these activities or the shroud may return. Although I will always be aware of what I can do, I also accept that as with all diseases I am not 100 percent in control of it and therefore it may return despite my best efforts. This is not my fault.

REBECCA L.

"Tell them to look up. Tell them to remember the stars." Renee Yohe's words made me believe hope is possible.

Looking back, I thought I could control when and where and how much I cut. At first, I could. But then the blade started to control me. My mind told me I needed the release to get through the day. It got to the point where I was cutting multiple times a day for a fleeting sense of relief. The scars gave me a sense of purpose and reminded me that I deserved what I did to myself.

My appetite for destruction could not be satiated; I longed for control and the feeling of ecstasy. I developed bulimia and anorexia.

My attempts to "control" my uncontrollable life backfired. I got so obsessed with controlling my appetite that starving myself and binge-eating were the only options left.

Last summer, I gave up all hope. I wrote letters to my family and had a plan to end my life. I stole some of my father's morphine pills and was going to take all of them on my birthday. I didn't want to commit suicide, but I wanted the pain to end. With my last ounce of hope, I told my therapist about my suicidal thoughts and behavior. Three weeks before my birthday, I was hospitalized. The first day was the most difficult. I didn't want to follow a routine or participate in group therapy. But I needed those things in order to survive my stay. I admit that the two weeks I stayed there put things into perspective. It didn't solve all my problems, but I was reprieved from them for a short time. I wish I could say all my issues magically disappeared. They didn't. I still have them, but I'm dealing.

For the longest time I never thought I would make it to eighteen years old. Now that I have come this far, I'm going to live my life to the fullest. And I will be happy while I'm doing it.

MELISSA M.

I am still here. Still alive. Still breathing. My packaging's a bit damaged, but I promise you I'm still worth the same. These marks that grace our bodies tell our stories and give us character. I don't mind them at all. However, I refuse to force that character upon myself ever again. I will take cuts and scars and bruises and burns from an adventurous and lovely life, but never again will I take them from the monsters that love to reside within me. I will battle these bastards that I've lovingly named Depression, Anxiety, and Self-Harm. I will create rather than destroy.

I have quite the life before me, and I'm excited to see where it takes me. I'm going to be okay. These monsters are strong, but I promise you I'm stronger.

KATIE K.

When I first became depressed at the age of sixteen, I felt ashamed by it—and by the fact that I couldn't make myself feel better. I tried to pretend for a long time that I was happy, that there was nothing wrong with me. But when I got to college, it finally caught up with me. I met with a doctor and began taking an antidepressant. I got myself more involved in my church and focused on leaning on my faith. My family was extremely helpful, too. I learned, in time, that my depression wasn't something that I should be ashamed of. It was a part of me, and part of what made me unique.

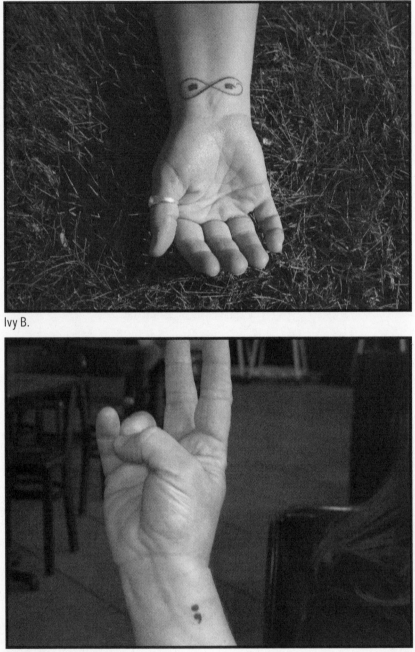

Ivy B.

Donna P.

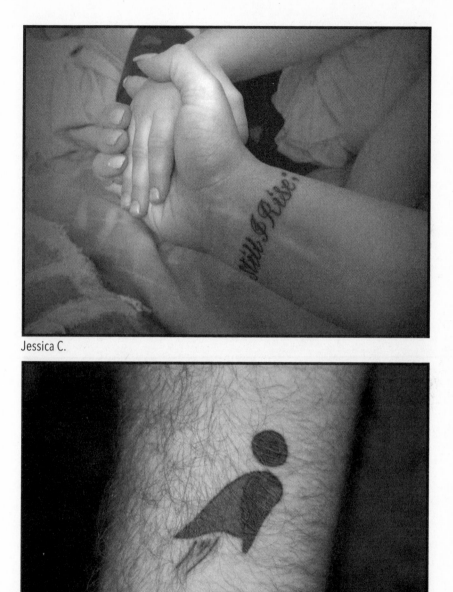

Jessica C.

Jim C.

RIINA H.

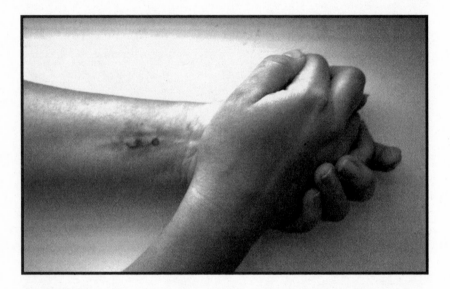

The people who know me would tell you I'm driven, open-minded, and straightforward—an entrepreneur and researcher in the health-care field. They'd tell you I'm a natural leader who cultivates loyalty and discipline, a person who is passionate about her work, strong and opinionated and unafraid to stand up for those who need it.

My brain does not agree with those people.

There's no reason why I should have severe depression and bipolar disorder, but I do. This has been going on for six years already, since my world was shattered by my parents' crazy divorce. The details do not matter. What matters is the fact that it completely changed my life. I did not have a home to go to anymore. My safe place was gone. This was the start of my escalation into the world where I live with depression and massive mood swings.

This year has been incredibly hard. I had periods when I could not even move from my bed for weeks. I did not speak with anyone, I was sad, annoyed, angry, and then . . . nothing. I just existed. I'd rarely eat, or I'd find myself binge-eating. I had massive tremors, anxieties, and times when I'd feel as if I was gasping for air, drowning on land. One of the hardest things to accept is that my issues seem trivial. I don't have an actual *reason* to wake up this way each morning, so different from the perky, happy person I used to be.

What I have come to realize is that I matter. It's me who needs to understand why I feel what I feel, why I do the things I do. You can lean on others at times, but true strength comes from within.

KATHLEEN B.

While other girls were obsessing over clothes and celebrities, all I could think about was why I felt so profoundly sad all the time. How could they focus on shades of lip gloss when it was all I could do not to lock myself in my room all day and cry?

In seventh grade, I liked a boy. I liked him so much that I gathered up my courage and told him so. He did not return my feelings, but he did take advantage of them. He knew I wouldn't tell anyone when he did inappropriate things to me under the lunch table, or at parties, or when we were hanging out after school and his mom wasn't paying attention—basically any time we were alone (and sometimes when we weren't).

I couldn't understand how he could treat me that way, how he could ignore my protests, how he could hug me afterward and call me his best friend. He told me not to tell anyone, because it was "our little secret," and because they wouldn't understand. I should be happy anyway, he said, it's not like I was the type of girl that boys would ever date. He told me I was too ugly, too emotional, too fat, "too much to handle." I couldn't make sense of the situation, and I felt more different than ever. At that point, I didn't know that sexual violence usually happens at the hands of someone you love. I thought I should just be happy that someone I liked was paying attention to me.

That summer came and went, and he decided he didn't need me anymore because he'd found another girl. I completely lost it when I saw them in the hallway together. I went home that afternoon and tried to end my life. Suicide was something I had been seriously considering for a while, and this seemed like just the push I needed. I took a bunch of pills, but as I sat there, crying and waiting to lose consciousness forever, I realized that I didn't want to die—I just wanted the pain to go away.

I made myself throw up, went downstairs, and told my mother what had happened. I was admitted to the adolescent psychiatric ward at the local hospital, where I stayed for a week. I'd like to say that it helped and my life was changed—but honestly, I think the only lesson I learned that week came from my hospital roommate, who taught me how to cut myself. That became my go-to coping skill, and there were periods of time where I was cutting every day. I met another boy and fell in love, but he ended it because I was afraid to have sex—a fear I now realize I carried with me from that first boy. My heart broke all over again. Any progress I had made toward healing was lost.

It became clear to me through my experiences that a survivor of sexual violence faces a very unique type of pain. There is violation, betrayal, instability, confusion, and often love—a love that logically should disappear when that person does something so heinous, but it often doesn't. The more research I did on sexual violence, the more I realized how serious, how tragic, how severe this problem was. I made a decision right then to take my life back by working to help other survivors take back theirs. There is no one better suited to wade through the murky, difficult, unspeakably painful aftermath of sexual violence with someone than another person who has experienced the same kind of pain.

In that moment, I morphed from victim to survivor. I went to college and graduated with a BA in psychology, then went immediately to graduate school and earned an MA in counseling. I landed my dream internship at a local sexual and domestic violence agency and could not believe how much it fulfilled, excited, invigorated, and empowered me. After graduation, I got a job there. The only word to describe how I felt was jubilant. I had endured so much over the years, and it had all paid off. My passion for survivors has continued to grow and change, and with all the recent focus on the epidemic of campus sexual assault, I have transitioned into a similar but new and exciting role. I now serve as the victim advocate at a large state university, where I counsel and advocate for survivors every day.

I used to think the world would be better without me, but now I like to think the world is glad I'm still here.

CINDY W.

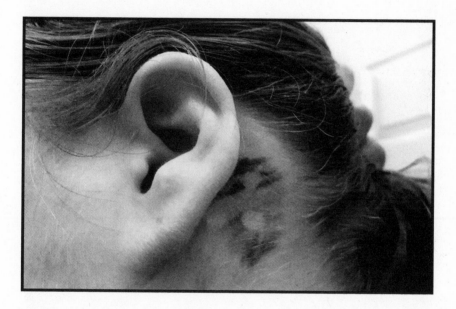

My experiences have taught me that everyone fights their own battles, big or small, and others will always feel pain and hurt differently than yourself. So, always be kind, even if someone is suffering from something you may find childish, because to that person, it could mean their world is falling apart. We all need to be there for one another and be judgment-free.

SARAH K.

When I was eight, there was a popular commercial on television for an antidepressant where the narrator explained the symptoms of depression. Seeing the commercial and hearing the symptoms made me realize that what I was feeling had a name. I found comfort in knowing I was not alone, and that there was help for people who had depression. When I got the courage to disclose my feelings to my parents, I was told I was "too young to be depressed." From then on, I suffered in silence.

At the end of my eighth-grade year, I attempted suicide. I remember being rushed to the emergency room by my parents and having to spend the night in the hospital. I can still remember the doctor coming into the room to explain that I could have died of liver failure. He added how painful it would have been, and what would have happened to my body, but he never once talked about depression or asked me what made me want to take my own life. He treated me as if my suicide attempt was nothing more than a cry for attention.

I started talking to a therapist, even though expressing my feelings made me feel weak. A part of me was still hoping the way I felt was just a phase; and by speaking my feelings aloud, I was afraid I'd be admitting it wasn't.

As I started college, things began to look up. I found a way out of my unhealthy relationship, learned more about my passions, and discovered a new group of friends. I thought that everything was going to be okay, and that my depression was in the past . . . but my suicidal thoughts crept back in, and my self-harming became worse than ever before. Finding myself at rock bottom, I broke down and told my therapist everything. I was committed to the hospital right away, where I was prescribed an antidepressant and given intensive therapy. Once I was discharged, I thought things would get better. But it wasn't long before those feelings of self-hate came right back, which resulted in me self-harming again. I checked myself into the hospital for the second time.

I began taking an interest in psychology, hoping it would give me the chance to better understand myself. I wanted to know everything there was to know about depression so that I could gain a deeper understanding of what I had experienced for so much of my life. After I was discharged and back at school, I took a leap of faith and enrolled myself in multiple psychology classes. With the help of therapy, the correct medication, and a strong support system, I realized that mental illness is just as real and serious as a physical illness. It was not all in my head, like I had been led to believe. I was not a weak person for feeling depressed, and it was not my fault that I felt this way.

I am proud to say I am two years self-harm free. But my story is not over yet. I continue to regularly see a therapist, work on my coping skills, and ignore intrusive thoughts that could lead me down the path of self-hate and self-harm. I surround myself with people who I can count on for support, and who want what's best for me. Oddly enough, I am thankful for my struggle. Without it I would not have discovered how strong of a person I am. I will not allow my depression to defeat me, or define me. I know that my battle is not over, but I will win this war.

TREVOR G.

Two years ago my little brother was diagnosed with anorexia. I watched him spiral downward for a year and a half, until he was skin and bones. The disease took over his body and mind. He was depressed beyond belief.

I have had my own battles with depression. They got worse when I went to boot camp last year; I had to come home. I felt unworthy and unfit for this life. I tried doing things to help me move forward and forget what happened at boot camp, but it was hard. My brother was sent away to Seattle to get help in a treatment center for eating disorders. My parents were sick with worry for their boys and would have done anything to help us. When my brother came home he seemed better, but that didn't last long.

On November 20, 2015, my baby brother took his life. The pain I have had to bear without my best friend is excruciating. In the six months he's been gone, I have gone through unimaginable anguish, torment, and pain. There have been days I wanted to give up and join him on the other side. I have wanted to leave this world, but I haven't because I see that life is worth living. I see the horror my brother's death has caused my family. I have seen my mom melted into a pile of sadness on the floor and haven't known what to do to help. But now I do know how to help. I know I can help by living my life, by finding joy and looking for the things to be grateful for. I can honor my brother and the battle he fought by continuing that fight for myself.

SAMARA J.

There was a time when I really believed this was all life had to offer. Death, despair, hurt, anger, darkness. Never-ending darkness. I saw a black hole in front of me. I was teetering on the edge. Constantly circling around it. Wanting so desperately to just fall into it, but something was holding me back. It was a constant balancing act.

I don't know when it changed. I cannot pinpoint the exact time, day, or even month. I was finally feeling fed up with being empty, feeling like I wasn't living. I started reaching out for help, more so than I ever had before. Started to take time for myself. Not much, a few minutes a week was all that could be spared, but it started to make a difference.

And then, at first, the meds were a huge relief, comforting almost. They allowed me to feel nothing. NOTHING. I couldn't even cry. I couldn't make myself cry. I couldn't scream. I felt completely numb. And in the beginning I was okay with that. That was all I had wanted for so long, to just stop feeling sad, lost, hopeless. To be devoid of all emotion. I had to be in a comfortable place mentally before I could begin to feel again. Little by little things started to come back to me. A tear shed when my son told me he loved me. Happiness feeling the warm sun on my face. A sense of calm while reading a book.

I started to realize that I could do this. I could learn to live and not be afraid of the everyday. Even though I struggle every day, I don't allow myself to slip back toward that black hole. I am not healed yet, and I may never fully heal, but I have come too far to give up.

JESSICA A.

I was the happiest child; I absolutely had the best family and loved my life. I played sports, had loads of friends, and was just a happy person. The first couple years of high school were all right, until my school closed down and I had to go to another school. The next two years straight, I was bullied endlessly by the popular girls, to the point where I started faking being sick just so I could stay at home in bed. At school, I would eat my lunch in the bathroom or in the psychologist's office, bawling my eyes out. Night after night I locked myself in the bathroom with a razor. I would sit there wanting to hurt myself, wishing I could end it all, but something would stop me. *You're too weak to even hurt yourself,* I thought, and my self-loathing worsened.

When I left high school, I started hanging out with an older girl I met at a party, and I got into a different scene. One night we went to a party that I don't remember much about, but I do remember waking up in a man's bed. There was blood on the sheets, and I was in a stranger's house. I called my friend, who told me that I had "begged" her to "let me go home with him." She later admitted that she had slipped me a drug to help me "loosen up," as apparently I was acting miserable at the party. I never consented to have sex with this man. He returned to the bedroom, and when I saw that he was about twice my age, I freaked out and left. I knew I had been sexually assaulted. I never consented. I never told anyone. I just left, caught a bus home, and lied to my parents about where I had been.

After that, I retreated even more within myself. I felt so alone in the world. I started eating when I was bored, happy, angry, sad, or lonely. Food became my comfort. Nobody even knew how I was feeling, because everyone thought I was the bubbliest, happiest person from the outside. I got extremely good at pretending.

I started dating a guy who asked me to move in with him after we'd only been together a month. I jumped at the chance since, initially, he treated me like I was his princess. I truly believed he was the one for me. The day I moved in, everything changed. He became abusive. He picked on my insecurities and started to play mind games. At first I thought I was being stupid and overreacting, but it worsened. He belittled me and my body. The emotional abuse continued, and he alienated me from my friends and family. I had no money to move out, and nobody in my life knew what was happening because I barely spoke to anyone. He was clever like that. Eventually, when he was at work, I told Mum what was happening, and we planned my escape so I could get out of there.

Though I was living with my mum and free of the abuse, my depression worsened and so did my anxiety. I barely wanted to leave the house. I would cry over nothing. People didn't know what to say to me. I didn't know how to function, because I hated myself. I believed everything my ex told me, including that I was nothing. I started to think maybe that was why I had been bullied in high school. I was stuck in a world where I felt I wasn't worthy of love or affection, and despite my family trying to convince me otherwise, I just couldn't believe it.

Today, I have a job I love. It's the only thing that keeps me sane. I am on a high dose of antidepressants to get me through each day. I've experienced several challenges over the past few years, and despite the fact that at times I didn't think I would make it through, I did.

I'm still here.

JULIETTE REILLY

have always turned to songwriting to get me through life's toughest challenges. When I've had a really bad day, sometimes the only thing that gets me out of a funk is sitting down with my guitar and writing out my feelings. Learning to write for myself and not for anyone else has become increasingly important.

High school was very rough for me. I was friends with a group of girls who were really mean. Their self-esteem was low and since I was always with them, this took its toll on me. And then I had a boyfriend who I dated off and on for five years who was pretty emotionally abusive. There was a month where I didn't come to school. I was never suicidal or involved with self-harm, but I was on antidepressants for a while. That was one of the darkest times for me. The only thing that really kept me going was one friend who really struggled with self-harm. She needed to spend some time in rehab while we were in a show at school together. She was away for over a month, and she still came back! She was stronger afterward, making me playlists of songs she thought would help me through my breakup and my struggles at school when everyone turned against me. What she did kept me going; here was this girl who almost died, twice, and if she could get up and come to school every day, then so could I! We became best friends and still share our songs and struggles to this day. She inspires me, as do a lot of people in my life, to keep telling the stories that need to be heard.

Facing my fears through song encourages me not only to confront my demons head-on again and again each time I perform them, but also to love myself for having the courage to get it out there. It's important for people to know that just because I don't post videos of myself crying, or when I'm at my lowest, doesn't mean I'm always happy. I want people, especially young girls, to realize that they are not the number of followers they have on Twitter or the number of likes they get on their Instagram posts. What defines you are your character traits, your heart, and your passions.

My goal in life has shifted from wanting to become a famous pop star to first and foremost wanting to be a role model for young girls. I want to encourage self-love and positivity on my YouTube channel, and continue to refine my craft as a storyteller. If I can inspire just one person to stop self-harm or keep going when they want to quit, my heart will be full.

> *You are not your mistakes, you are not your past, you are*
> *not the kids in high school who said you'll never last.*
> *You are not your parents; you are not your good-byes. So*
> *before you give up this fight, I hope you realize you can be*
> *your own hero.*
>
> —*"Hero"*

CHRISTIAN B.

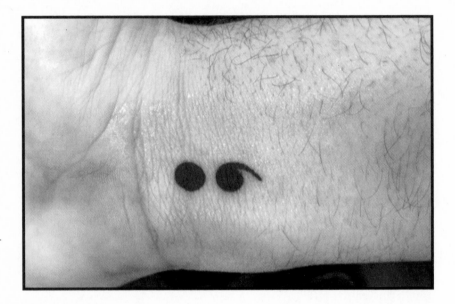

During the nearly twenty-five years that have passed since my military service with the United States Marine Corps, I have felt something was terribly wrong with me. Yet I believed I was hiding it well. My nightmares, self-isolation, consumption of drugs and alcohol, and heightened sense of alertness (including barricading the door to my house and other erratic behaviors) were classic symptoms of PTSD, but I did not want to acknowledge that I had a problem. I thought what I was feeling was weakness, that I wasn't being tough enough. PTSD often happens when you're too strong for too long.

As time progressed, it became apparent to me something was not right in my internal world. Though I got married and the next year I was blessed with a son, my newfound happiness could not overcome the pain I felt inside. One Saturday morning, my son wandered into our room to get into bed with my wife and me. I was groggy after another restless night of intermittent sleep and nightmares. Startled by my son, I awoke abruptly, ready to defend myself. I grabbed his wrist very hard as he moved in the bed. Though I scared myself more than I scared him, I realized my panic attacks and disconcerted state of mind were something I had to address.

A few days later I walked into the Disabled American Veterans office. I started therapy and now, less than three years later, I feel that I am becoming a less dangerous man every day.

If history has taught me anything, it's that we are all undefeated when it comes to getting through bad days. It may not be easy to think that way when you feel like the walls are falling down around you. You are stronger than you think, but that doesn't mean we can't use some help.

EVE R.

I can recall the precise moment when I remembered I could laugh. I was sitting with my best friend, who eventually became my roommate and remains like a sister to me today. We had purchased giant wineglasses, and as we were chatting at the dining table, she tipped hers up to take a sip. Her face, distorted by the bottom of the rounded vase and sloshing wine, struck me as the funniest thing I had ever seen, and I began to uncontrollably ugly-donkey-guffaw laugh until my face was equally distorted in mirth. It took me a full half hour to calm down, because every time either of us picked up a glass, it started me off again. It was *wonderful* to laugh.

It was a silly moment, but it gave me hope. I am so lucky that my family and friends have always encouraged me to look for hope. My psychiatrist tells me I have to take credit for surviving, because however incredible my passengers are, I'm still the one driving. I love the metaphor, but I'm pretty sure that having people you can trust to drive when you can't made all the difference for me.

I am loved—so very loved, so very lucky. And I am enough.

AARON P.

I've visited Rock Bottom so many times over the past eight years that I've begun to make friends with the residents there. But even though I get to see my "buddies" every time I travel through, it is definitely not a place I like to stay for very long. Sometimes, my visits are short and sweet, and I catch the out-of-town bus with a smile and a wave. Other times, I cannot seem to leave. I have to sleep in the shadows, under the weak glare of the street lamps, waiting for somebody to come along and help get me the hell out of there.

Before I began treatment, I was a boy on a tailspin to absolute oblivion. At the time, I was trapped in a seemingly never-ending cycle of bad days. For no apparent reason, I woke up every day terrified of what the day would bring. I was exhausted with irrational worry over everything happening around me. I wasn't eating. I wasn't sleeping. My self-esteem was stuck in Rock Bottom. I often kept my head down as I went about my day, just wishing I could go back home and lie down in the security of my bed. One night, a thought came racing into my head: suicide. It scared the crap out of me. I came face-to-face with oblivion; I held my fate and future in my own hands. The next day I decided to get the help I needed. I immediately got in touch with a social worker and began weekly therapy sessions.

Going through treatment has taught me a lot about myself and the world around me. I've learned so much in these past four years that, weirdly enough, I'm almost proud of the darkness I've had to crawl through. These battles have hardened me. I'm scarred and bloodied, but I somehow cannot stop smiling. Having an anxiety disorder has taught me about empathy, sacrifice, loyalty, trust, and determination. I've had more second chances over the past few years than many have in a life-time. Having to brush yourself off after falling is never a fun thing to do, but it shows an inclination to fight like hell to live the best life possible.

There have been plenty of hardships along the way as well. I've relapsed into darkness more times than I can count. I've had those scary thoughts of oblivion enter my head three more times since the first. I lost a girlfriend who I felt was unwilling to understand how anxiety impacted my behavior and who could not continue to support me in my fight. I've had to deal with times of complete helplessness and loneliness. I've had to break down and collapse, then turn right around and rebuild time and time again.

Despite all those hardships, I have transformed into the man I know I was supposed to become. I am an advocate for the voiceless, dedicated to making the world a more empathetic and helpful place for those who need it most. I've taken tremendous strides toward my career goal as a police officer. I've sculpted a support system that is the strongest it has ever been in my twenty-two years on this planet.

I've adopted Project Semicolon's message of continuing on as a personal message of hope. I chose to keep fighting. I chose to rebuild. I chose to live.

Keep fighting. Keep supporting.

Love.

A little bit goes a long way.

REBECCA H.

I used to think your disease robbed us of our childhood, the kind of sepia-tinted memories we should have made growing up on the old farm at the end of a dead-end street all the neighborhood kids thought was haunted. We let them think it was. And maybe we believed it, too, traipsing through the woods around the house, searching for something we couldn't name but could feel vibrating in the air just beyond our bodies.

But the truth is, we weren't robbed. We were blinded. There is a reason our instinct as humans is to squint against the intrusion of sudden light when we are in the dark; it's because the truth is overwhelming. Often, it hurts.

The first time I discovered you cutting, I was nine. You were eleven. You asked me not to tell Mom and Dad because it was your secret. I was no rat; I understood we were allies. "When everyone else is gone," Mom used to say when we came to her, bickering, "you'll only have each other. Don't forget that." I didn't forget, and so I kept your secret.

Years later, when your disease erupted in a mushroom cloud of devastation over your first semester of college, I thought back to that day—to finding you on the couch in the basement, slicing the word "asshole" into your arm—and regretted not telling someone. I learned a hard lesson that day, a bright and blinding reality: you wouldn't always be able to save yourself. And by keeping your secret, I had kept those who might have saved you in the dark.

You struggled. The medicines that kept you from wanting to die gave you migraines that reminded us your brain would always be a saboteur, a source of pain and anguish one way or another. But you persevered. You became someone who, despite her rocky path, found happiness. Real, honest-to-god happiness. You were so happy, I let my guard down. I let myself believe it could last forever.

Last night, when I got the call, I felt my legs go numb. The realizations came in waves: You waited until your husband was out of state for work. You waited until our parents were gone for an overnight trip to the city. You left a note, your will, and your fourth-quarter tax returns on the kitchen table.

You really meant it.

I know it's not that you don't love us. I know it's your disease, the insidious, many-tentacled thing lurking in the down-deep, always waiting to wrap you up and squeeze until you breathe your last. Knowing doesn't make it any easier to think of you cutting long furrows into your wrists.

At the last minute, you got scared. Who wouldn't be, watching the water in the tub darken to a harrowing shade of crimson. You called someone. The police came. They saved you this time. *This time.*

We had our eyes opened a long time ago, you and I. But remember, my love, that we're supposed to have each other when everyone else is gone. We have to look right into the sun and dare it to blind us. We can't settle back into the dark, complacent. You belong here, with me—with all of us. We love you. Always have, always will.

A.M.

I t started when I was young, around five or six years old. An older
boy who was being babysat with me asked if I wanted to play "doctor." Excited and intrigued, I agreed. I didn't know "doctor" involved
pulling down my pants, but that's what happened next. Day after day,
I actually asked to play doctor with him, thinking it was normal. My
brother was in the basement with us, and he obviously knew it was
wrong; he told my parents and eventually our family lost contact with
that individual.

Fast-forward about seven years and I was off at camp—a two-
week cadet program on a military base. I met a boy. I thought he

was cute and we hit it off. What I didn't know was that he started his games the moment we met; he lied to me, telling me he was thirteen. I later learned he was older. Less than two hours after we met, he was demanding kisses and had his hands down my pants and up my shirt. I reported him to the camp counselors, who asked if I wanted to press charges. That sounded scary to me at age thirteen, so I refused. Instead I buried the whole incident. The camp legally had to inform my parents, so they did. I called my mom on the phone that night. She said we would talk when I got home. That talk never happened. It was as if the whole event never happened.

Ten months later, I started cutting. At the time, I didn't know why, I just did it. My very first cut was with broken glass, but not just any glass. I'd broken one of my dad's empties and carved into my own emptiness.

I quit the cadet program after two years; it was a decision I would come to regret. At eighteen, I moved out of my parents' house because I couldn't handle the effects of my father's alcoholism, or the emotional and verbal abuse. Finally, frustrated with life, I realized I couldn't keep cutting. I reached out. I sent a message to my dad asking if we could talk sometime. His response? "If it's about that boy at camp, just forget about it. Move on, it's not a big deal." My world crashed to a halt. My father, the man who was supposed to be my hero, had let me down. *How can he say that?* I thought to myself. *It's not okay. It* is *a big deal!* I was so upset, I threw my phone at the wall.

That day is significant for me, because it's the day I learned a lesson I know I have to share. DON'T EVER MINIMIZE SOMEONE ELSE'S PAIN; it DOES matter. If a person cannot cope with a difficult conversation, help them find the right resources (counseling) or at least give them a hug! If you are reading this as a survivor, know that there is no severity index for sexual assault that dictates how you're supposed to feel or allowed to feel. Sexual assault is never okay. For the longest time I felt insignificant, like what happened to me didn't matter, like I wasn't allowed to be upset (YOU ARE ALLOWED TO BE UPSET). I don't hate my dad, in fact I love him very much; I know he didn't intend to hurt me, but he did. I've had to come to terms and accept that my dad will never be the father that the little girl in me needed.

So, how did I heal? I reached out to others who were capable of being emotionally present for me. I went to counseling and did some hard work. I stopped cutting and now I share my story publicly through writing, speaking, and volunteering. I've returned to my old cadet squadron to finish what, earlier, I wasn't able to.

I received a medal from the military camp that in some ways tells the story of my journey. *Ad Astra Per Aspera*, it reads—"Through Adversity to the Stars."

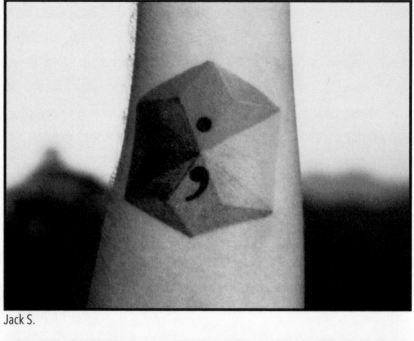

Jack S.

Lex A.

Marcie C.

Mel T.

NICOLE B.

It was summer. I spent my days at the New Jersey shore, soaking up the sun and hanging out with my friends. I came home one night to find the TV wasn't on as it usually was; Dad wasn't sitting in front of it and Mom wasn't flitting around the kitchen, chatting and cooking. Instead, my dad was just sitting in silence, staring at nothing. He said, "Nikki, come sit down, I have something to tell you." I sat down, not knowing what to expect, but sensing something was very wrong. "Grandma"—his mom—"died today. All of us will be staying home to be with the family." He shed a few tears. I stood up, gave him a warm hug, and felt my head melt into his chest. I told him I loved him. I smelled the stale odor of cigarettes and the peanut butter and Ritz crackers he was eating on his breath. I didn't want to let go, but I did. I was scared. I had never seen my dad so numb, torn by such sorrow, so vulnerable. This wasn't the man I knew, the one who could talk to anyone, the man who made you feel like you were the most important person in the room, the man who everyone wanted to be around.

That was the last time I spoke to or held my father.

Later that night I woke to my mom screaming, "Nicole, call 911!" I ran into their bedroom. My dad looked like he was sleeping, but my mom hovered over him shaking him. He didn't move. I called 911. I called my best friend and asked her to come over because my father was sick. The ambulance could not find the house—it was a new development—so I ran outside in my underwear and flagged them down. It must have taken fifteen minutes. The EMTs started CPR; they put my daddy in the ambulance and drove away to the hospital.

By the time the ambulance arrived at the hospital, my dad was dead.

Life changed. I wore a bright red-and-orange dress to the funeral because that was what my daddy would have wanted me to wear.

My mom became chronically depressed; I was left to care for my two younger brothers. It was my senior year of high school.

I was angry. I went to school but very rarely to class. Days were spent in the parking lot smoking cigarettes, or climbing up on the roof of the school to sunbathe. Someone had decided I was too fragile to "handle" being on the varsity cheerleading squad, so I found other ways to get boys' attention, even if it was in the woods behind the athletic field. I took pills, who knows what kind or how many times. I wanted my dad back. I wanted my mom back. I started a pattern of inpatient stints at psychiatric hospitals and was awarded a diagnosis of bipolar II disorder, rapid cycling. I stopped the meds again and again because the colorful cocktails would numb me, make me not feel, make me not myself.

In my midtwenties, I lived at home with my mom. My little brother was away at college. He started calling home, speaking oddly. He said he would go out and strangers would start talking about him and they would say he was sick. A white van would follow him around all the time, and the aliens would read his mind and hear his thoughts. Eventually, it scared my mom and me so much, we drove out to Pennsylvania to see him for ourselves. He was sick, talking to himself, hearing voices, cursing loudly on the street in response to threats only he could hear. He was diagnosed with schizophrenia and, after being in and out of various psychiatric hospitals, was eventually committed to a state institution where he spent the next two years of his life.

My little brother's diagnosis changed me. I still struggled with my own bipolar, but I felt I was stronger and better without the medication. I liked how fast my mind could go; I liked that I was smart, that people couldn't keep up, that I was interesting, that people wanted to be around me and know me. Inside I was a complete disaster.

I applied for a job in human services as a residential home manager for adults with disabilities and mental illness. I had no experience, but I had conviction and the spirit, drive, and will to make a difference. When I was offered a chance, I took the job—and found my calling. I learned how to care about people in a way that I didn't think was possible outside my own family or selfish, attention-seeking agenda.

I still have bipolar. I still battle the mania, and I still have days where I am too depressed to get out of bed. But I found medicine that worked to control my symptoms without making me feel like a zombie, and just as importantly, I met my husband. He is the man my life longed for, the one who grounded me and loved me at my worst. We have three children, and they are the air that I breathe.

I am proud of my struggles. They no longer have to be kept bottled up, something I can't speak of, something I have to hide. They are part of me—but they do not define my future.

JENNIFER F.

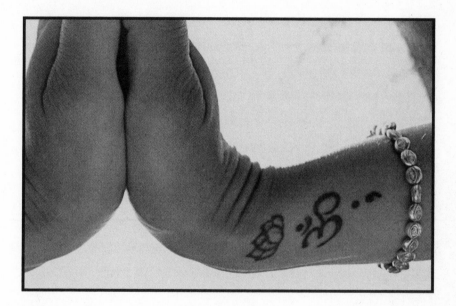

Rewind to 2012. It's a new school year, I'm twenty-four years old, sitting in a classroom with eighteen-year-olds. "What am I doing with my life, why am I so far behind?" screamed the demons in my head, day in and day out. I'd go home, back to my parents' house, feeling like I'd lost all control. I felt like I should have had a career, an apartment, a life partner, and a solid core of friends by now. I could check one thing off that list: I had a great boyfriend, and I was lucky for that—or so I thought.

Eventually, I realized I had little control in that relationship as well. I was insecure, lost, and in the shadows. I needed something that could be mine and only mine.

I found exactly what I was looking for.

Once I started, I couldn't stop. I eventually told my boyfriend, who insisted I tell my parents. They didn't get it, no one did. *Just eat. Snap out of it. You look great how you are. Where did you learn to do it? What did I do wrong? What is wrong with you? But you love food. You have such a great life.*

In comes my dad, the smartest, most understanding man in the world. He was completely clueless about why I would be doing it. But he assured me that I wasn't behind anyone in life—I was simply exploring all of my passions and ensuring I found the right one. Apparently, it is common to feel this way at my age, not entirely happy or confident in where you are in life because you expected so much more from yourself. Reality takes time, and success takes hard work and patience. Don't worry, he'd tell me; you'll find your calling soon. Don't worry.

Less than a year later, I found myself single, depressed, and not wanting to make much effort in my social life. Sad, right? The only thing I had going for me was being thin. Finally, I had control over something—my body! I could wear whatever I wanted. I felt confident in a bikini or crop top. I was getting compliments wherever I went. There was no better feeling than that. *Wrong.* It was easy (sometimes) to put on a happy face, but no matter how I looked, nothing changed the fact that I still couldn't find happiness, acceptance, or just shut off all the demons in my head.

I made my way into therapy, which has been life-changing. I

realized I was emotionally abused in my relationship. Shamed, name-called, controlled, threatened, excluded, demeaned, disrespected, and cheated on—just some of the things I let him get away with. I was diagnosed with depression, anxiety, and "It"—the demon in my head, an eating disorder.

Today I don't even recognize the person I just described. Sure, the antidepressants help, but so have the hours of therapy and damn hard work. I think of the girl who was caught in that relationship as a completely different person than the woman I am today. I've also found a lot of calmness, comfort, and peace with my mind and body image through yoga and meditation. Never hurts turning to the big man above, as well. I put a lot of my faith in Him. Lastly, it is with utmost excitement that I can honestly say I have found my worth. I just finished my bachelor of commerce degree. I have a set career path, reconnected with and met some of the best friends I could ever ask for, and a family (and dog) who are my biggest fans and support group. I could not be happier with my life.

I will never again let anyone treat me as less than I deserve. I know my value and what I have to offer. The self-respect I have for myself will not allow me to settle for anything less, ever again.

GERALD M.

I was abused, I was alone. I stole, lied, spent most of my days and nights stoned . . . I loathed myself, and I hated what I had become, the awful things I did, my selfishness, the way I treated others.

Depression is a darkness with no doors or windows. I blamed everybody else for the empty shell I had become. I overdosed many times, then spent two years in rehab to end my chemical romance.

It took a long time, but now I'm here. I really feel alive. I wake up early, open the curtains, see the new day, and *feel*. The last time I tried to kill myself was two or three years ago . . . I overdosed and woke up in the hospital. But something has changed since then. I don't blame anyone anymore. I want to be here. God has always been waiting in the shadows and touched my heart and showed me something new. I am alive. I am learning to smile again.

CHELSEA W.

Even before I moved away from home and into a shared house, I had extremely low self-esteem and high self-doubt, and I was plagued by a constant stream of suicidal thoughts. I started drinking alcohol so I could forget; I'd stay up all night smoking cigarettes and only sleep when the sun came up.

I decided I needed help and I told my mother about it. She recommended I go to the doctor. I booked an appointment that morning and had a massive breakdown. I felt that I was worthless and a waste of space, and that my whole family would be better without me. The doctor sent me to the hospital. The very next day a mental health nurse came to see me; once again, I lost control and cried my eyes out because, obviously, something had caused this.

After about the fourth day in the hospital, I was transferred to a mental health unit. I thought I didn't belong there, with people who were coming off addictions and beating their partners, people who believed in things that aren't real. The first time I saw the psychiatrist I said there was nothing wrong; I'd never cut myself, though I had always had these suicidal thoughts. They increased my medication and soon after sent me home.

I went back to the mental health unit three times after that first admission. Now I'm back to work, taking my medication, and talking to a mental health nurse. I keep thinking I am doing better, but I am never sure. All I know is that my story isn't over yet.

SABRINA T.

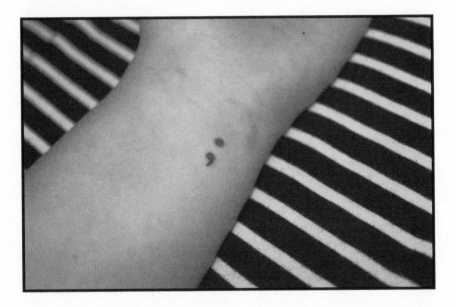

In the beginning, the black dog was small. He kept me up at night; I struggled to fall asleep and stay asleep. Soon he blocked me from going out. I didn't want to socialize, and I didn't enjoy the activities I used to love.

Then suddenly, the dog had grown to werewolf size. I was in a constant state of sadness. Everything felt impossible and I wanted so badly to give it all up. I had no will to live. I hit rock bottom. I was self-harming daily, drinking until I blacked out. I was a mess.

One day, a friend asked simply, "Are you okay?" It was like she had leashed the beast at last, and dragged him a little ways off my chest.

She convinced me to get help, and though it hasn't been easy to find the right medicines, I've managed to find some that keep my mood somewhat stable. I still have my down days, but my mood is nothing like it used to be.

My therapist believes my depression has come from years of suppression. From years of childhood bullying, abandonment, divorce, academic failure, and my fear of disappointing the people around me. Life hasn't always been rainbows and butterflies, but I hid everything I could to seem stronger than I actually was. Inside I was struggling beyond words, but I didn't want to be weak.

What I know now is that you have to be the strongest kind of person to seek help. You are not a failure, you are not weak; in fact, you are strong and you should be so proud of yourself.

No one truly knows the power of the three words "Are you okay?" but those words are the reason I got the help I needed before it was too late. You don't need to say much to make a difference. Just three simple words might even save a life.

LAURA T.

In Memoriam

In 2011, Scott, my older brother and best friend, jumped off the roof of his fourteen-story apartment building. He lived—his heart was still beating—but he would never be the same person again.

Neither would I.

Within nine months, Scott would wake up from a coma, be diagnosed for the first time as schizophrenic, and successfully take his life on a subsequent attempt. My family and I were left with the stark reality that our brightest star had been extinguished.

Losing Scott was the biggest tragedy I've ever experienced. Trying to get past the pain to create something beautiful was both harrowing and necessary. I knew Scott wouldn't want me to get lost in grief, no matter how easy it was to slip into darker places.

Since Scott's death, I've dedicated my life to doing what he once told me to do: know what you love, never forget it, and be brave enough to do it. We each have something special to share with the world, and we're all here to help each other take those bold steps forward.

ALYSSA B.

I sat on the psychologist's big leather couch, knowing that many others had also been here before me, crying to her. I was fifteen years old, and I did not want to be like the others. I wanted to be strong. I wanted to prove that I was different, that nothing was wrong with me. I explained to the psychologist how I had been feeling. She wrote down every word I said, all the while wearing a look of concern. I was proud that I'd told her my feelings without a single tear, until she asked me a question I was too ashamed to answer. Had I ever cut myself? The tears came flooding out. There was no longer a need for words; she had her answer.

It was on that day that I was diagnosed with depression and mild anxiety. I kept my disease hidden from everyone else, including my family, as best as I could. I knew that if others found out, I would be judged and ridiculed.

I was dating a guy who turned into someone I felt I could trust. I let myself grow closer to him, hoping my disease would heal. He noticed one night that I was upset and quiet. He asked me what was wrong, said he noticed I'd been "different" lately. Only I wasn't different; this was my normal. I trusted this guy and knew he cared for me, so I let my depression, finally, reveal itself to him. I could see the confusion and shock on his face. I put my head down, thinking all my fears of being judged were true.

When I started my senior year, I was still suffering from my "made-up, dramatic sadness." In my Anatomy II class, our assignment was to write a paper on a disease and what area of the brain was affected. From previous counseling sessions, I knew depression was caused by a hormone imbalance, but I never researched the specifics or causes. I asked my teacher if I could write about depression and she said yes. I researched for hours, reading and learning so much I never knew. I was amazed by the facts. Depression is caused by hormone or chemical imbalances that affect the neurotransmitters in our brains. The research also said that people with depression have no control over it; it's a real disease, a mental illness. This definition was based on facts.

When it was time to present our projects to the class, I was very nervous. I feared being laughed at or called "dramatic" again. My face got hot and my palms were sweaty just thinking about it. When it was my turn, I stood in front of everyone and read to the class my personal thoughts and how I had been affected by this disease. I then explained what causes it, the symptoms, cures, etc. When I finished reading my report (and crying, too), my classmates applauded me. I was stunned. My teacher said something when I finished speaking, words I will never forget. She said, "Society treats depression or other personality and social disorders so much differently than a disease like autism. Why? They both are out of our control and caused by defects in the brain. People with depression suffer just like those with autism, Alzheimer's, or dementia. We need to stop judging and viewing it as a made-up disorder and more as a disease." Her words allowed me to at last achieve a feeling of acceptance.

I haven't self-harmed in one year, three months, and twenty days, and I now look back on my depression as a semicolon—just a pause in the sentence of my life.

I now know that I can continue on.

ANGELISE S.

My story starts in summer. A friend and I were in the car on our way home. I don't know how we got on the topic, but I mentioned that the sound of fingernails clicking together bothered me. My friend then proceeds to click her fingernails in my face and said, "Like this?" Yes. Exactly like that. I felt such a rage deep inside me, all from a sound. That was the moment I realized something wasn't quite right. A few months later, I ended up seeing an audiologist because my family thought something was wrong with my ears. "She has misophonia," the doctor told us.

Misophonia translates to "hatred of sound." But I prefer its other name, selective sound sensitivity syndrome, or 4S. I don't hate all sounds, but I have a severe sensitivity to most human-based noises. My main triggers include sounds of eating or drinking, the aforementioned fingernail clicking, and sounds related to the nose and mouth. Some of my triggers bother me so much, I can't even say or write the sound because it brings up the sound immediately in my mind. I also can't look at someone eating or drinking because I can imagine the sound that goes with it.

After that summer ended, I entered my freshman year of high school with a clear understanding that I had a rare disorder. My reactions to an ever-increasing number of triggers went from annoyance, to fleeing from anyone who made sounds, to crying, to hiding in my room with loud music, and eventually digging my fingernails into my palms and arms in order to distract myself from sounds while in a classroom. I didn't know how to ask for accommodations at school because I couldn't think of anything that would help me. It felt stupid to say "sounds bother me." My family tried to help, but they didn't understand what misophonia really was, and I didn't know enough about it to express what it was like. I was the cause of a lot of stress and friction in my house. I broke the tradition of eating dinner at the table with family because it was torture for me. My mom couldn't understand because she was hung up on the idea that I was scared of sounds. We fought a lot because I would refuse meals with the family, then later go eat on my own. I avoided eating while my family was awake, eating at night so I wouldn't get yelled at.

Senior year it got pretty bad. Even though I knew that it was misophonia that made me act and feel the way I did, I still questioned my sanity. One day, I was at an all-time low and questioned whether my life was even worth it. My dad found me sobbing and realized how bad things had gotten. He made me a promise that during the summer, we would find a way to make things easier. My mom ended up finding a couple of videos about misophonia that explained it in ways I couldn't; she finally started to understand what I was living with and why eating at the table was so painful for me.

Even though it was hard, I graduated with honors. I had also been accepted to my number-one choice of college, University of Georgia. While I was extremely excited, I was terrified of large lecture classes. I could only imagine all the sounds I would hear during the winter:

coughs, sneezes, sniffing, and other triggers. At orientation, my dad attended the Disability Resource Center's session. I spoke to a coordinator and expressed my insecurities; she told me about the paperwork I needed to get and promised she would work with me to identify accommodations to help me get through college.

I have bounced around to different doctors trying to find something to help me gain some control in my misophonic life. Thus far, that has included medications and biofeedback training. During therapy, I was also diagnosed with anxiety, depression, and possible post-traumatic stress disorder. Everything that happened in the past is in the past, but moving forward, I will try to have nothing but strength as I work toward getting better.

ROSE O.

I've been in a constant war zone with my mind since I was in high school. But it all started way before. I was emotionally, physically, and sexually abused by my family from the time I was very young, though it didn't really hit me until I was in middle school. I had just moved to a new place for what felt like the fiftieth time; I didn't know anyone and didn't fit in, even when I tried to act like the other girls. I became depressed because I had no friends and I lived in a home where abuse constantly happened. I had no refuge—no safe escape.

The older I got, the worse my anxiety became. I'd feel a tinge of panic when I needed to go out, even just to get the mail or take out the trash. Anxiety caused me to feel stuck. I ate constantly to cope with the stress of living in an abusive home, and the weight gain made me feel very fat and ugly, and on top of that, my family criticized me about it. So during my sophomore year, I felt very ashamed of myself. I didn't look the way I was supposed to and my grades were nothing but Ds and Fs. I felt so bad about myself that I thought, *I deserve to get hurt.* I wanted to feel in control of my pain, so I got a knife and slit my wrist. It hurt, but at the same time it was so relieving. The cutting got so bad that I had to be admitted to a psychiatric facility for self-harming and suicidal thoughts.

And you know what? I actually really liked it in there.

I was around other kids who were like me, and I didn't feel so alone. But I had to go home, and when I did, things just got worse. To this day, I still struggle with self-harm. I feel like it's the only thing that gives me the release I need when I feel like the world is against me.

Living with depression, anxiety, and self-harm tendencies is really hard. Having to live with borderline personality disorder on top of that is a lot harder. I knew there was something wrong before I was diagnosed. I'd love someone one minute, and hate them the next because they looked at me funny. I'd spend money excessively on things I didn't need, to the point that I almost became homeless. I began a reckless lifestyle that involved a lot of sex, drugs, and money. I just started to feel out of control; I had no idea what to do anymore.

Thankfully, I'm no longer living that life. I walked away from the bad influences and put my partying days behind me. I decided to get baptized and started walking with God again after many years of atheism, and it has made me a lot happier and stronger.

Regardless of how my past looks and what I struggle with, I've become a stronger person. I've realized my worth and know that I have a lot to offer to the world. I'm still recovering from past wounds and my heart is still healing from all the cracks, but light is definitely shining through them.

DOROTHY Y.

My life took a turn for the worse when I tried to take my own life. After overdosing on alcohol and prescription drugs, I was intubated for thirteen hours. I could not breathe on my own and was hospitalized for five days, followed by a stay in the psych ward. I didn't want to die, but I didn't want to go on living the way I was either. I went to treatment at a center in Illinois, where I met the most incredible woman. I can proudly say that I have been sober from alcohol ever since. With her support, I have been able to fight my addictions and discover a life I knew could be worth living.

MARJAN R.

I was angry with the world. I was angry with the circumstances I'd been dealt and the emotional neglect I seemed to constantly feel. My pain was invisible, a battle hidden from the world around me.

My depression was an uphill battle I fought alone out of fear that I would be alienated from the community I had worked so hard to build for myself. I suffered in a dark internal isolation, smiling on the outside, hoping to never burden anyone with my struggles, thinking that was the truest form of strength and leadership. *You can't tell them you're depressed,* I told myself. *Be strong. Fix this yourself. No one cares about your sadness. You have everything in the world you could ever ask for. Stop crying. Get a hold of yourself.*

Ten years ago, I made a commitment to myself to be healthy. I looked down at my arm, staring at the wounds I had given myself, hoping I would feel something and that I would regain a sense of control. I didn't feel that. Instead, I felt sadness and disappointment and promised myself that was the last time I would ever self-harm.

Most people don't know about my depression or self-harm because they only know the girl who grew into an optimistic, fun-loving young woman. I have learned that feeling sadness, anger, and pain is okay and healthy; finding joy, peace, and adopting a new reality is okay and healthy too.

I will never get to erase my scars, and I will never be able to undo all of the moments that have made me feel too weathered to be compassionate. I will, however, keep moving forward on my journey. I will keep finding peace in these moments and with the person I have become. I will keep trying my hardest to offer kindness to those around me, much like everyone who has offered me an unbelievable amount of love and strength amid their own struggles.

If ever you feel alone in this world, seek out support and love yourself. If ever you catch yourself projecting your anger, undeservedly, onto others, take a breath. Remind yourself that they, too, are human and fighting their own hard battle.

HEAVEN-LEIGH S.

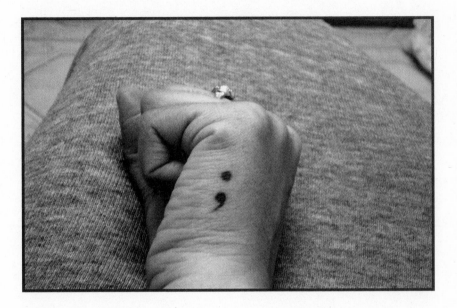

Every day is a struggle, but then again, every day is a triumph—just to be alive and see another day.

Things may get harder for me as I get older, but I know one thing for sure: my fight isn't over. I am ready. I am building my strength to keep moving forward.

K.J.

When my mother called to tell me my best friend had been hospitalized after attempting suicide, I was calm. I knew she'd be okay. I mean, they found her just in the nick of time. She'd pull through and we'd laugh about it later.

Or, that's what I thought.

Khanya was my best friend. We'd been friends since we were toddlers, and our bond stayed tight as we grew up, even when we went to different schools. As the length of her hospitalization extended, I grew impatient and anxious. I started to believe what everyone was telling me, that the overdose caused a lot of damage and she wouldn't make it. I started to give up on her. I started to make peace with the fact that I would never know what drove my Khanya to the point of deciding to end her own life. The idea that one day I'd get answers slowly started to fade.

Day in and day out, I visited the hospital. She was in a coma for a long time. Eventually, the doctors ordered her mother to take her home because there was nothing they could do for her anymore. Helpless and hopeless—that's what I felt.

I started visiting less. You see, the pills had done so much damage to her nervous, muscular, and motor systems that she was there but she wasn't there. She wasn't . . . *isn't* Khanya anymore. She can't walk, talk, go to the bathroom . . . her condition became unbearable to witness. I try to force myself to visit regularly, though I don't know why. Every time I go, I discover hope I didn't know I had before— hope that she's still going to get better. But no, every time I'm met by a blank expression and a few inaudible moans and groans. I leave hopeless again.

I used to call her cell phone, just to hear her husky voice on her voice mail. I haven't heard her speak in seven years. I've stopped calling. It has been like grieving someone who is still alive. But I'm trying . . . we're all trying to make peace with it still.

Now it is like we are living a life that continues as it should, but one that is stagnant at the very same time. It shouldn't be this way. I feel that she selfishly left us to pick up the pieces. I wish she could have trusted me enough to tell me what was going on. It could've helped, you know? Khanya's incident has taught me the true meaning of having to forgive someone who hurt you without understanding why. I won't lie, I am still extremely bitter, but I am nonetheless trying to move on, to push through, to continue.

KAITLIN S.

When I came clean to my first serious boyfriend about my self-harm, he came clean, too—about the fact that he was only dating me to feel better about himself. The relationship ended quickly and I spiraled down into darkness, angry with myself that I had tried to be normal, that I tried to reach out about my issues. A couple months later, I met my best friend, my rock, and the love of my life. What started as him just wanting to help me feel better became so much more. He helped me realize that I had so much to live for. We have been dating for about three and a half years, while I have been completely clean from self-harm for about two and a half years.

On a regular summer Tuesday last year, I was coming home from my boyfriend's house, where I'd spent the day. I pulled into my neighborhood behind an ambulance and a fire truck. As I drove to my house, so did the ambulance. And as the ambulance parked in my driveway, I sprinted into my house with the EMTs. My body was numb as I saw my stepdad lying on the kitchen floor. I'm studying to be a doctor, and I knew what it meant when they said my stepdad had no pulse and no brain activity. I wanted to tell them to stop, but all I could do was hold my mom and tell her it was going to be okay while they took him to the hospital. They tried and failed to revive him for forty-five minutes. I had lived with my stepdad for twelve years.

He was perfectly fine, and then all of a sudden, he was dead with no warning or reasoning at all. I didn't know how I should feel because feeling doesn't come easy to me, but I knew things would never be the same.

Even though some days are really hard, I know it'll get better, and I have a lot of support in my life from my friends and family. There will be bumps in the road, and life may be tough, but I'm tougher, and I am loved.

STEPHANIE C.

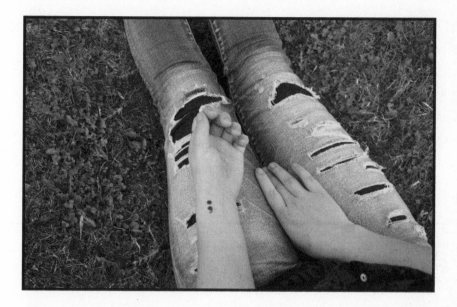

The bullying started in elementary school and came from people I believed were my friends. I began to believe that cutting my wrists was the best chance I had at feeling anything other than emotional pain. My parents thought I was going through "a phase," and it seemed like they never knew I was struggling with very real, very dark thoughts.

One day I just broke. I was rushed to the hospital due to an overdose on my antidepressants. That was the night my life changed forever, and for the better. I had hit rock bottom, which now I realize is exactly where I needed to be. My true friends and my family dropped everything to help me get back up onto my feet, to help me stand and figure out my new life.

I was diagnosed with bipolar disorder. Alongside medications came life changes. I began to put myself first. I began to take care of myself in ways I had never believed necessary before. I began to live in a way I was proud of.

My life is in no way perfect all of a sudden; I still have days where I want to relapse into my old habits. But I find ways to remind myself that my life is better now than it was before. The people I surround myself with are the reasons I am able to be strong and discuss my struggles. They remind me of the things I love and am passionate about, and they love me a little harder on the days when I'm not feeling up to being 100 percent myself.

Yes, the medications help. But if it wasn't for the positive energy from my friends and family on a daily basis, I don't believe I would be where I am today.

JOSHUA D.

B *oys don't cry. Men don't feel.*

These are messages I grew up hearing and believing. So when I started to feel certain ways about myself and my appearance, I knew there was no way to express it. I didn't look like the buff leading man in movies; I saw myself as ugly, someone not worth noticing. By not eating, I thought I could improve my self-esteem and make myself look better.

That part of my past is a blur, a lot of black and a lot of darkness coating what everyone told me were supposed to be the best years of my life. But between hating myself and thinking about taking my own life every day, I knew that these people had no idea what they were talking about. Days turned into nights and nights turned into days, but the gray I felt inside stayed the same.

I never thought that mental illness might be in my cards until a year and a half ago, when for three weeks straight, no matter what I was doing, I felt like bursting into tears. I knew I had to see my doctor—something wasn't right, and if I didn't see someone I wasn't sure what would happen.

My diagnosis shocked me; I felt embarrassed. *Men don't have eating disorders,* I told myself. The small number of friends I told were surprised because of my outgoing personality, which was something I always had, but when I was at home or alone I crumbled into myself.

Everyone I told was supportive and wanted me to know they were there for me. I knew there would be people who didn't know how to react and I was fine with that; I wasn't relying on anyone to help or fix me. I'd never really had anyone there for me before, so I wasn't looking for that after my diagnosis. But to my surprise, some people stuck by me then and have hung on ever since.

My family hasn't responded the way I thought they would. It's not their fault if they don't know what to say, but not saying anything at all is the worst thing to do. But by talking about how I've been feeling and my experiences, I've been able to create my own little family of friends who are always there for me, even when I don't expect them to be.

Mental illness is perceived as something taboo, something that should be swept under the rug. But it's quite the opposite. You'd be surprised by how much people are willing to listen, and how much they want to learn about what someone they love is going through. Being in the dark felt like my life until I let in some light. I know that even on days when I feel like giving up, the people who love me are championing me to keep going.

CHARLOTTE W.

I was fourteen years old when my sister was sexually assaulted. Over the next few years, my parents gave her all of their attention. My brother and I just existed on the side in our own separate ways. He was angry; I was stone-cold silent.

After transferring to a private high school, I was still very depressed. I often thought about suicide and figured that everyone would be fine without me. I self-harmed because I wanted to be in control of something in my life; I was held on such a strict schedule because of the way things had gone for my sister. I thought that nothing would ever become light, and I couldn't remember the last time I'd been happy.

But happiness was just around the corner. At sixteen years old, I met the love of my life. He came out of nowhere and surprised me with open arms. He has the warmest heart, makes everyone laugh uncontrollably, and will do anything for the ones he loves. I call him my angel, because he saved me. But he wasn't the only one: I saved myself.

In college I met some incredible friends who inspired me to share my story and come forward to my family about everything. I also found the courage to come out to my friends and family as bisexual. I was finally free of my personal chains and felt invincible.

I am proud to be alive today. As my favorite quote states, "I want to live, not just survive." And that's exactly what I plan to do.

JULIE C.

If you are reluctant and do not try, you may not get anywhere. Once I shifted my focus from things I couldn't control to things within my control, my life improved. I took it one step at a time: I got a job so I could have money, so I could save up to move out of my parents' house. After that, I started taking online college classes. All of this took time. Nothing changes overnight. Progress will happen, slowly but surely. It is possible if you put in the work and take it one step at a time.

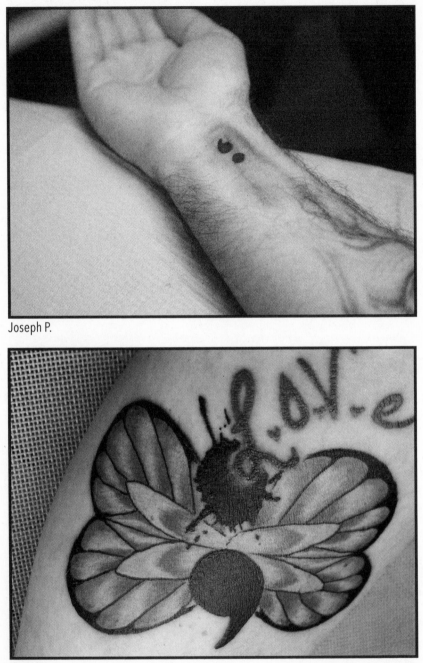

Joseph P.

Kristi W.

Libby (for Dylan xx)

Michelle A.

DOMINIC L.

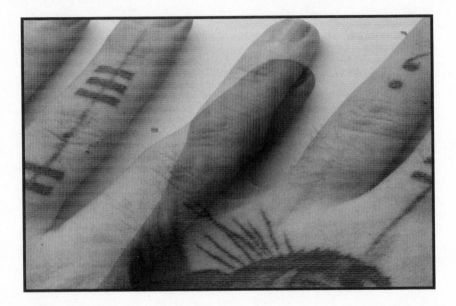

heard the first voice when I was thirteen. It simply whispered my name. I didn't know hearing voices was "abnormal" until I was twenty-seven, the age at which my whole world tipped completely on its head.

What started as a cry for help to my doctor resulted in assessment after assessment, each resulting in a new label being stuck to my existence. Borderline personality disorder, dissociative disorder, schizotypal, schizophrenic. With each new diagnosis I watched as my friends started falling away until, on the eve of starting my treatment program, I found myself facing the hardest journey of my life without any of the people beside me who'd said they'd be there.

Therapy began, and it was not pleasant. Within the first weeks all my defects were brought to my attention and I felt subhuman, useless—and the voices had fun confirming all that negativity, increasing in volume and depriving me of the mental space I needed to focus on getting better. It was too much, and one day it all poured out to my therapist, whose stunned silence spoke a thousand words. When I was offered medication to help quiet the voices, to create space to concentrate, I agreed to try it on the condition that the meds didn't sever my connection with my reality completely. But the medication took away everything, and the resulting silence was deafening.

The change caused me to break down completely. Every piece of the reality I had existed in since I could remember was snatched away and I couldn't cope with the world that replaced it. I spiraled down-ward. Every day for months, the only thoughts I had were of suicide. I started making plans, saying good-bye to loved ones. When I went to my mum's for Christmas, in the home I had grown up in and where this had all begun, I put my plan to overdose myself with heroin into action. When the needle was in my arm, my best friend was finally able to get through to me and provide me with some light to strive toward. It is because of her that I'm still here to be able to write this. With her help I managed to drag myself out of the hole I was in.

Five months later, just as I'd reached a point where I was looking toward the future again, tragedy struck: my best friend died. While we were alone together in my flat, she had a heart attack and, after calling the ambulance, I had to perform CPR. They were unable to revive her. She had saved my life, but I was not able to save hers. I had lived to see my savior die.

In her memory, and because I knew she wouldn't want me to do anything else, I continued to push forward with my treatment in the hope of becoming the better, more stable person she had been looking forward to seeing at the end of my intense therapy. I wouldn't let all of the effort and support she had channeled into me be for nothing.

I got a semicolon tattoo to represent my struggle with, and survival from, depression, suicide, and addiction. It is my promise to be true to myself in both good times and bad, and to try and learn to love and respect myself. Throughout my life there have been plenty of times I could have ended it, either through my own wishes or the commands of the voices I hear, but each time I chose life. I will always choose life.

KERRI B.

I noticed throughout college that my anxiety was triggered by exams and my performance in school. I had always been pressured to do well in school, and when I didn't perform well just one single time, I developed anxiety about all kinds of tests and exams.

I am an avid animal lover, so I started reading up on emotional support animals. I decided to get a rabbit. He helps me feel relaxed and improves my mood. Now I know that no matter what life throws at me, I can do anything I set my mind to.

MENACHEM R.

I believe that hope is everything.

I used to find hope in the smallest things: a good grade, a friend's smile, my faith in God. But all that changed when I was fifteen and my sister passed away. . . .

In that moment, I lost everything. I lost my innocence, my trust in God, and my childhood. Even hope. I became severely depressed for many months. I refused to eat, go to school, or even attempt therapy.

Over the next five years, I lost all hope. *All* of it. I sat on my bed, very depressed, unable to imagine life ever getting better. I sat there with a handful of random pills in one hand and a letter in the other, contemplating suicide; I saw no other way. But then a miracle happened and a glimmer—a tiny, tiny glimmer—of hope emerged, and I made a phone call. When no one answered, I made another call, and another, and another. Finally, I got someone on the phone and he talked to me for forty-five minutes while I cried. And those tears, mixed with his voice, created for me a new hope.

Hope flushed the pills down the toilet. Hope sends me to therapy every week. Hope gets me out of bed every day, ready to battle for my happiness. To me, hope is the most important thing in the world because without hope, everything else is worthless.

I once came across a beautiful quote: "*Hope* stands for 'hold on, pain ends.'" I agree completely. Hold on. Just keep going, because this will pass and it will get better. Just have hope.

EMILY T.

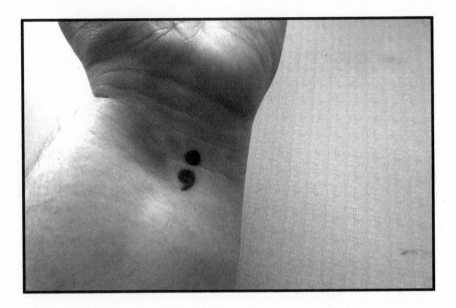

Though I had struggled with anxiety and depression since my early teenage years, things truly came to a head when my husband and I started trying to have a child. I went off my medications, because I was afraid the drugs that kept me in check would harm the baby. What followed was a long struggle to get pregnant, each month harder than the one that came before. Each month, when my cycle arrived, I would spiral down into a deep depression. I felt like a failure.

After seeking medical intervention to become pregnant, what should have been a joyful, long-awaited experience turned into my own personal nightmare. Medical issues, as well as my own demons, plagued me. I rarely slept, ever fearful that my child would slip from me as I slumbered. Finally, I was placed on a low-dose antianxiety medication halfway through my pregnancy.

On a cold March morning, my daughter came into the world a month early, with a head full of dark hair like her father's. When I held her, I cried both in joy and fear. What was this tiny human? I was so scared of her, of the responsibility she represented.

That gave way to resentment and anxiety, and a crushing sadness that I was terrified to express to others. Because I was supposed to be jubilant, to know what I was doing, to have my instincts rally to the forefront and lead me into motherhood. Instead, I was in a state of exhaustion from trying to breastfeed, because that was what was "best" for all of us, and what mother doesn't want to give her child the best?

Slowly, over the next two months, I continued to spiral down. I refused to acknowledge how sick I'd become for fear of losing others' love or support. I started an antidepressant as soon as I was discharged from the hospital, because I knew in my heart and soul that I could no longer deal with my illness on my own. Though my husband, friends, and family were and are incredibly supportive, I refused to tell them the dark pain that lived in the back of my head. I never told them that I was jealous when my spouse went to work, or envious of other mothers who talked about how good their babies were when mine was screaming fifteen hours a day with colic. I was determined to provide breast milk for my daughter because I felt I couldn't, absolutely could not, fail at this one thing. But it was hard, and painful, and I was exhausted.

Finally, at my daughter's eight-week checkup, I sat in front of her doctor and I cried. A dam broke and I cried and cried because I felt like such an absolute failure, adrift in an ocean of my own making. Calmly, the doctor said that she believed what a child needs most in the world is a healthy, present parent. I was neither.

On that day, I turned a corner and sought help for postpartum depression.

My story isn't over. I am still here. I am walking a hard road, but the miles are adding up. I asked for and received love and support, and I got a small spot of ink that reminds me every day that I am still here. That I can, and I have, gotten better. That my daughter will know that even on the days I struggle, and the days when getting up is hard, that she is so, so loved. You, reader, are loved. Never doubt that.

ASHLEY G.

When I was eighteen, I got pregnant. Very soon after was the first time he hit me. He would choke me and punch me in the head so that people wouldn't see the bruises. He would make me have sex with him even when I was too tired. He has broken my hand twice, broken my nose, knocked me unconscious, given me black eyes more times than I can count, and spat in my face and held me down while it dried on my skin.

I've had blackouts. I've cut myself. I developed an eating disorder. I've had suicidal thoughts . . . but I am still here. When I found myself feeling completely empty inside and unable to get up out of bed, I knew there was a problem.

For me, treatment was really just in time. We really need to get the facts out about treating mental health instead of covering it up. Thank you so much for giving me the opportunity to speak about this.

JADE C.

My parents divorced when I was twelve, but that wasn't before my father's violent, alcoholic abuse had taken a toll. Living in that house, I had learned to fear everything. I was afraid of my own voice. I wanted to disappear. I also wanted to control something in my crazy-out-of-control life. I became anorexic at the age of nine. I was introduced to alcohol in high school and it became my best friend. Alcohol destroyed everything about me and around me. I was an empty shell.

I decided that I needed to get help and was committed to an alcohol and drug rehab program, where I got sober. I stayed sober for two years, but the pain of all the childhood abuse was too much to bear. I started drinking and using again. I took myself down a deep, dark hole, ruining myself and my life as I knew it. I attempted suicide seventeen different times. Finally, after ten years of the darkness, I was sick of it, and sick of myself. I needed to get out.

I got help. I went to Alcoholics Anonymous and have been sober since. I have a life now beyond my wildest dreams, and I'm not going anywhere.

JENNIFER D.

High school was the worst time of my life. I was bullied and told to
kill myself every day. The teachers did nothing. My mum went to
the school about it and got the answer "Kids will be kids."

There was no safe haven for me because I also lived with a mentally abusive family member. I got into drugs and started to self-harm.
I attempted to take my life three times.

I succeeded once. I was dead for two minutes. But I survived.

During my first year of college, I broke. It was reading week and
everyone was gone and I felt so alone. I contacted one of my teachers
and, with her help, I started on my road to recovery. Two months after

my major breakdown, I met an amazing man who helped me turn my life around. With his love and support, I got the help I needed. From going to doctors to opening up to my mum, he was there by my side. We will be married two years in December.

I'm over a year self-harm free. I'm happy. I'm in love. It does get better.

KAT G.

In Memoriam

The tattoo is for both me and my friend. We were students in theater together and had been battling depression. We had both, at times, planned to end our lives. We found out about each other's depression and told each other we were okay and not to worry. Two weeks later, as we were opening a show, she ended her life. This tattoo is in memory of her and her beautiful soul. It's a reminder to keep going and to be sure you find your light.

MEGHAN K.

Before, it was like I was drowning. I couldn't breathe, everything was foggy, and no matter how hard I kicked or splashed, I couldn't get my head above the water.

I managed to break the surface, but only halfway. I could see daylight, but I still couldn't breathe.

I kept treading water until the waves rose above my nose, and eventually my whole head. The ocean is still there, right below my chin. I can see sharks swimming by. They don't tear at my flesh like they once did, but they still bump into me with sandpaper skin, leaving me with small scars that need time to heal.

I long for the dry, grass-filled prairie I know God inhabits. There are no sharks there. The sun shines there, warming me with His love, and the wind blows, taking away unrest.

I'd like to punch those dumb sharks in the eye so they swim away and never come back, but remember, my arms are still submerged. They move so slow even though I want so badly to make a swift escape. There is no fast moving when you are underwater. It's all slow motion, turning impatience into insanity.

I've been in the abyss. I've been so deep that not even the sharks can stand the pressure. There's no light there. I cried out to the Lord, "Save me, O God, for the waters have come up to my neck. I sink in the miry depths, where there is no foothold. I have come into the deep waters; the floods engulf me. I am worn out calling for help; my throat is parched. My eyes fail, looking for my God" (Psalm 69:1–3). He did save me; I truly believe that. He has no limits, yet I am still surrounded by water.

There is no quick fix for this. No yacht, cruise ship, or even rescue dingy in sight. I dream of a strong arm reaching over, pulling me up and out of the water, then letting me rest in the sun until I am healed. No matter how many times I dream this dream, in the water I remain. The sun shines and I have many good days in a row, standing in the sea with the rolling waves of life. But there are still the sharks, waiting for the clouds to come out when they can sneak up on me unannounced. I am never safe. I am constantly vigilant.

"But I trust in your unfailing love; my heart rejoices in your salvation. I will sing the Lord's praise, for He has been good to me" (Psalm 13:5–6).

ALEX S.

At the age of five, as I played and smiled with my friends in the neighborhood, I was struggling with questions deeper than the holes we were digging in our sandboxes: *Why do I barely ever see my dad? Why are my parents divorced?*

I thought the answer was simple: me.

Believing it was all my fault led to me continuously cry myself to sleep for the next decade. Finally, when I began high school, I felt as if I were on the same playing field as my classmates as we entered those halls as freshmen. I soon realized that although we were all dealing with physical changes in our bodies, many of my classmates didn't seem to be dealing with the same emotional instability I'd been feeling for the past ten years.

The one area of my life where I did see stability was football. I had played every fall since second grade. Football wasn't affected by what apartment I lived in, where my dad was living at the time, or even my emotional well-being. It was as if my helmet protected my brain from the negative emotional thoughts being introduced to it. Playing football through high school was a great experience. It encouraged me to question and try to understand the impact of my anxiety. How could I be cheered on and supported by more than one thousand students every Friday night, yet feel so alone around those same classmates on Monday morning?

At the beginning of my sophomore year of college, the harmful thoughts in my head transformed into harmful actions toward my body. I began cutting and harming myself, believing that I deserved the pain I dealt with when I was younger. This emotional stress soon led to physical issues, including a point where I was vomiting four times a day, every day. I was confused and frustrated that my body was able to rid itself of the food that purposefully entered only thirty minutes before, but still had difficulty eliminating the thoughts of worthlessness that had entered my brain without invitation nearly fifteen years ago.

I transferred schools junior year, joined an elementary education program, and was determined to turn my struggles into a success story. I started speaking out about my struggles, and tried to spread one critical message: You are not alone.

JESSICA G.

When I was seven years old, my father went to prison for inappropriate actions with my cousin. I was devastated. At that time, I didn't really understand what was going on, I just remember the police telling me to say good-bye because I wouldn't be seeing him for quite some time. After a while, my family began visiting him almost every weekend in the different prisons he was assigned to. I developed a strong resentment toward my father and the life situation I had because of him.

In junior high, I started hiding my feelings from my friends and family. I discovered a new "release" in self-injurious behaviors. For a long time, no one ever knew anything was wrong, while privately I experimented with cutting and other forms of self-injury on and off throughout the next few years. I was the master of the fake smile. Eventually my mother did find out. Though I insisted I would stop and told her I did not need to go to a counselor, I just learned to be better about hiding it and shut out even more of the outside world.

One night, as I sat with a blade to my wrist, ready to end my life, a friend sent me several persistent text messages. At that point, I was so vulnerable that I finally crumbled and let somebody in on my side of the very high, very thick walls I had built around myself. She gave me a glimpse of hope that night.

I continued to battle depression, cutting and doing other self-harming behaviors, but I finally had an ally . . . until she had heart transplant surgery. After that, I felt like I couldn't talk to her anymore. How do you talk to somebody who just received an incredible second chance at life about how much you don't want to live? So, I closed myself off again, and spiraled quickly downward. The cutting became very extreme and very frequent, and the suicidal feelings and urges were happening almost every night.

When I started college, my campus had a free clinic that included counseling services. After a great inner struggle, I decided that I didn't want to feel so bad anymore. I called to make my first counseling appointment. That call was the best decision I ever made.

In the midst of counseling, I had a terrible memory flashback that I had completely blocked out. When I was about four, my babysitter's husband had taken me into a room alone to "play" and proceeded to touch me inappropriately and stick his fingers in my private areas. Feelings ranging from embarrassment to disgust to shame flooded through me. This revelation felt like a huge setback in the progress I'd been making. I didn't sleep well, or often at all, for about a month, and some very strong urges kept pushing their way into my head. I dreaded going to bed because I knew it would be a battle for my life until the next morning, and then I'd still have to get up and go to classes.

I started hearing the suicide hotline rundown all around me, and have now heard it more times than I can count. I've dialed the number many times, but never hit send. I wasn't sure I actually wanted saving. Medicine helped tremendously, once we found the right one and the right dose. I know I gave my counselor a run for her money, but thankfully she stuck with me and I made it through.

This past January marked five years clean of any form of self-injury. I have come off medicine and, aside from the extremely introverted personality I developed throughout all of this, I am a very functional member of society. I'd be lying if I said depression and thoughts of cutting don't creep back in sometimes, but I have a wonderful support system. I'm thankful every day that God has given me a second chance at a good life and surrounded me with loving and supportive people who make me want to stay alive and well.

SURABHI S.

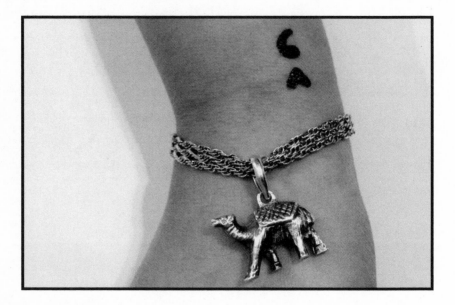

In Memoriam

My family was traveling by car, the four of us—my father, my mother, my younger brother, and me. We were going on a pilgrimage. It was early morning so my brother and I were asleep. It was Republic Day in India. The next thing I remember, I was in a hospital room. Many things were connected to my body. I was in an induced comatose state. The only thought I could muster was, *What happened?* I didn't even realize I had been three months in the hospital. For me, time was relative. It's surreal to me, even today.

My life is a miracle. Every breath is of gratitude to a higher power. I am still recovering. I am a work in progress. I learned the most important lesson yet. It is LOVE.

Love the life you have. It might not live up to your expectations now and again, but be forever grateful that at least you have a life. I lost my brother in that accident. My parents survived. He was my baby brother, and I can never get over his death. But I love him all the same. The thing about love is, it's in you! Not in any other person, or an object. It's always in the heart. It calls to your soul. Wherever you are, express love at all times. I don't have any regrets apart from that I didn't say "I love you, Yash" enough. I'm sure that he knew it. There was love in every gesture, even the way I would wake him up for school.

Yash lived his life king-size. I wouldn't have it any other way. It was love and purely love in everything I did for him. But I wonder, was it enough? For me, it's never enough . . . I have, had, and always will have unconditional love for him. He might have said, "It's a known fact." Almost as if it was a universal truth. It's like breathing. Do you say it? No, it's an unsaid emotion. It's intangible. It can just be felt when you love someone.

Sometimes I feel I have such a small time to gather my love and my loved ones. I feel like a lifetime isn't enough. I feel as though my soul is leaking with love and I don't know when it shall be over. At just the blink of an eye, it seems. I don't have time to take it slow. Little by little. Step by step. It's a hurricane of love that I feel around me. I don't know when it shall stop. But I pray to the Almighty that not a drop of my love should be wasted. Not even half. Life is too short not to love and be loved.

I did not lose the love I had, have, and will always have for my brother.

SOREN W.

My world had become bleak and broken. Heartbreak, the loss of a beloved pet, and weeks of solitude on the open road had nearly consumed me. Left alone with nothing but my thoughts, I spiraled downward. I had convinced myself that the only possible way to stop the free fall was to stop living completely. I had battled the waves before, but the combination of everything I was going through had created a perfect storm. I had lost all hope and was ready for the end.

But for whatever reason, the universe had other plans. Just as I reached my lowest point, I simultaneously met a new friend and reconnected with an old one. I would never have thought these two would become the support system they are for me, but they allowed me to be completely open and never passed judgment. They cared for me more than I'd ever cared for myself. And I'm forever indebted to them both.

ASHLEY L.

When I was little, we moved a lot. After moving to five different states in two years, we finally bought a house and settled down. Around then, I remember expressing for the first time that I was inexplicably sad. I didn't understand it, let alone know how to explain it, but it was there. The sadness just sat there for a few years, not overwhelming, but always there in the quiet of my mind.

When I was thirteen, I moved with my mom and siblings back to my hometown because my grandpa was dying of cancer. One morning as I was getting ready for school, I heard my mom yelling on the phone. A few minutes later she came into my room to tell me that my grandpa had committed suicide. I kind of went blank. I didn't know what to think or even *how* to think about what had just happened.

That was a dark year for me and my family, and that event was only the beginning. A lot of things happened, and the sadness I had begun to see years before was now undeniable. The pain left me hopeless. All the problems overwhelmed me and I thought that the feeling would never go away. That August, I tried to kill myself for the first and last time. If there is something that feels worse than getting to the point of wanting to take your life, it's failing at it; it was like I couldn't even do that right. Yet that event drove me to want to get better, and I spent the next two years climbing back up the ladder of hope.

By the time I was sixteen, I was doing a lot better. I had friends. My family was doing better. And then the floor caved in. A situation in our family did us all in. I didn't acutely spiral because I was still holding on to hope, but a slow, sneaky sense of apathy crept into my life, to protect me from feeling so much pain again. It became difficult to enjoy the good things. I couldn't feel anything if it wasn't boiling rage or unbearable sadness that made me cry until I screamed. I hated being that way. It scared me. I scared me. I thought I wasn't trustworthy with myself or others. I would hurt myself or hurt someone else because "hurt people hurt people" right? My hope was once again gone.

Eventually, someone talked to my mom about their concerns for me. She then asked me a question that has marked me ever since: "Do you want to get better?" I was so close to giving up, but the answer was yes. If there was absolutely anything I could do to get rid of the black cloud over my head, I was willing to do it. It took a few years to get what you could call "better," little by little, day by day. I had to learn to feel again. I had to face my pain and feel it, though not all at once. God has been by my side every step of the way and is the only reason that I made it through—and I did make it through.

HAYLEY P.

reathe, Hayley, breathe. I remember the first time I had to talk myself through an anxiety attack. *You're fine*, I told myself—but I wasn't. Not even the slightest bit.

For months, I went without help. The longer I went, the more it affected my work, my relationships, my health, and basically every aspect of my life. People often ask me why I didn't get help immediately. The honest answer is embarrassment. I always have it together. I am the smiliest person in the room, and I pride myself on being someone who is never negative, someone you can always look to for a good laugh. I honestly just couldn't fathom people seeing me in a different light or not being that perfect person.

So what did I do? I continued to be that person on the outside, but on the inside I was churning with anxiety and depression. It got to the point where I wasn't sleeping, ever. I was falling asleep during conference calls, and my relationship at the time was crumbling. I would lie awake at night, thoughts racing.

Eventually, people started to ask questions. I had become a walking zombie, and looked dreadful. I prayed and prayed for an answer, and then one day, it hit me like a ton of bricks. I got a phone call from a very dear friend who told me they had been battling severe depression issues and had gotten to the point of wanting to hurt themselves.

They were going to receive treatment. After that phone call I realized it was time to get help.

I had to be at my appointment with the doctor at four p.m. That day I was running behind at work and, simply because I was going to be a few minutes late, I threw myself into a massive panic attack. As I sat down in front of the doctor, she said, "Talk to me. What's going on?" When I started talking, I sounded as if I had chugged three Red Bulls just before I walked in. She stopped me immediately. I started to breathe heavily, and metaphorically the thousand-pound elephant sitting on my chest came back. I started to sob uncontrollably, saying "I can't do this anymore" over and over again. She calmed me down and spoke with me about the medicine that could help me sleep and prevent my anxiety attacks. She also scheduled me to follow up with a psychiatrist. I had hit what I thought was rock bottom. Little did I know how much further there was to fall.

I had seen the doctor, taken the first step. My next task was telling my family, my boyfriend, and my friends. I sat each of them down and explained to them what was going on and what needed to change in our relationship to get me back to me. At first, most of them were mad as hell that I hadn't told them sooner or asked for help. Then came the tears, and then "What can we do?" I couldn't have asked for a better support system. In the days following I received text messages from everyone almost every morning, telling me, *you're beautiful, you're amazing, you're such a strong person, keep your head up, you can beat this, don't give up*, etc. Looking back now, those text messages meant the world to me. They brightened my mind and heart, and helped me start off the day with a smile, as much as I still didn't want to.

Between the medicine and biweekly psych sessions, I began to see an improvement. The thousand-pound elephant started going away, and the light in my face started to brighten again. Just as things began getting back to normal, my boyfriend and I decided to split up. All at once, I took a million steps backward. I had lost my best friend, the bedrock of my support system, and the person with whom I had spent a majority of my adulthood. I found myself once again barreling down a bad path of depression and transforming into a person that I am ashamed now to even acknowledge. My coping mechanism became drinking a bottle of wine or two a night, until I passed out. Again, I was lost and embarrassed to ask for help. I began to lose weight quickly because I would rather drink than eat, or I would just sob until I was sick enough for my dinner to come up.

I finally hit bottom in the middle of a psych appointment, when I fell dead asleep in the middle of talking with my doctor. She shook me awake and asked what I had done the night before. I said I'd gone downtown till about four a.m. She looked me dead in the eyes and told me to come back when I was serious about getting better.

Feeling outrageously ashamed, I went home and cried, and prayed, and cried, and prayed. I grabbed the cross around my neck that belonged to my grandmother Mame. Mame was the strongest woman I have ever met, and she always taught me to be strong, to never give up. I prayed for her to send me a sign, and show me that everything would be okay. As I was looking up from my prayer, my dog, Lucy, jumped into my arms and licked my face. That night, anywhere I went, she went with me—and honestly, that hasn't changed over the last eight months. Of everyone, Lucy has been my saving grace, and I truly, truly believe that she was put into my life for this obstacle, as she was a stray that chose our doorstep to show up on.

After that night, I said to myself, *Hayley, enough is enough, get it together, you're better than this.* I called my psychologist the next day to make another appointment, and somehow by the grace of God she agreed to see me. We sat down, and all I had to say was, "Tell me what to do, I'm ready to be better." We talked about my plans for medication and therapy sessions, and I haven't looked backed since.

Don't be ashamed of your conditions. Go get help immediately, and don't wait because you're embarrassed. Don't fake happiness to please others if you're suffering on the inside.

I MADE IT OUT ALIVE AND SO CAN YOU! Never give up, and remember Jeremiah 29:11: "'For I know the plans I have for you,'" declares the Lord, "'Plans to prosper you and not to harm you, plans to give you hope and a future.'"

ALEXANDER P.

My story begins way back at my earliest memories. I remember being sent to my room for something I did. I'd lie in bed alone with nothing but my thoughts, always wanting to—and eventually attempting to—suffocate myself with my pillow. I carried on this way until my late teens, when the urges turned to hanging myself in the living room. This is an urge I always fought.

I thought that if I could get out of my household and have a family of my own, I'd be so happy. Well, as I got older, I grew angrier and angrier. I hated life, people, places, things. If I saw anyone being happy or smiling, I would cringe and get angrier. Thoughts of suicide came and went faster than ever. My midtwenties brought me my first son. Everything would be better now, right? Boy, was I wrong. Even when I had everything I wanted in life, I still struggled to pull myself out of bed each day and face the world. No one suspected any of my thoughts or feelings because as society sees it: I'm a man and we don't show our feelings.

About a year ago, I finally broke down and searched for answers and help. After all these years of fighting and knowing I was different than the "norm," I was diagnosed with PTSD, severe depression, social anxiety, generalized anxiety, and ADHD. I wear these labels like battle wounds; I don't show them off, but they will always be here.

DOT S.

It seems so strange to me now, that I tried to kill myself when I was seventeen. I was serious about it, too; I overdosed and ended up in intensive care. Doctors said if they had gotten to me just a few minutes later, I would have died.

I was messed up, and I could go into detail as to why I did it, how I did it, what I took, and what I remember, but I don't think I need to. The fact is, if you asked me exactly why I did it, I genuinely couldn't tell you. I had a lot going on at the time, and my head was just in the wrong place. I had school, I had exams, I was going through what everyone does. There was nothing out of the ordinary going on.

And in some ways, that's the most terrifying part of it all.

When I recovered and went back to school, there were rumors—jokes, actually—made about my attempt. People said I'd tried to do it with Tums. At the time, I laughed along, but now I look back and am horrified that this was considered acceptable. I don't think many people knew just how serious my attempt had been, but even so, suicide is not something that should be joked about.

I've come a long way since then; I finished my A-levels, did a foundation degree, married a wonderful man, had a baby, and am expecting my second. I can't believe I nearly had none of this. Things got better. They can always get better.

TIFFANY K.

I have to remember that tomorrow, this pain I'm feeling won't feel the same. It can get worse, but most of the time it gets better. Take a second to analyze your situation; that second can make all the difference. Understand others, understand situations, and most of all, you must understand yourself.

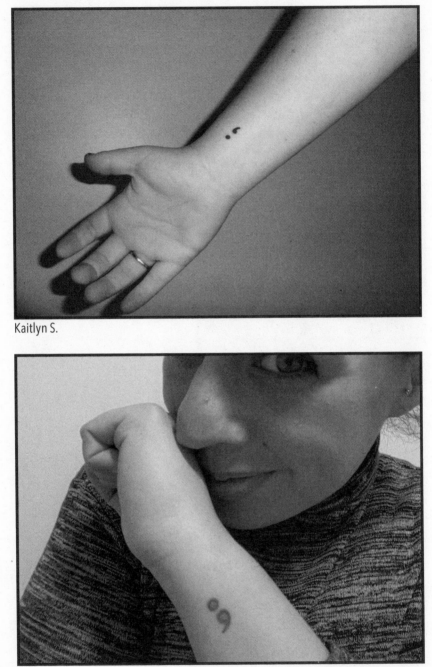

Kaitlyn S.

Sammy H.

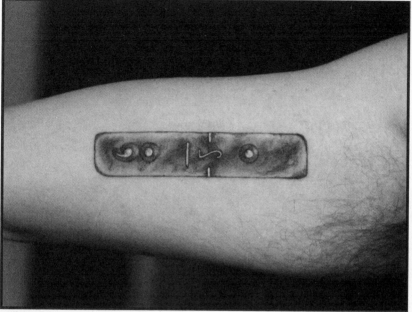

William D.

Rodolfo F.

APRIL W.

I was an only child. My dad wasn't around often and he spent a lot of time at the bar. My parents decided the older couple across the street from our house would be a better fit to watch me.

I don't remember how long it was before the molestation started, but I was around six or seven when I was sexually molested by my babysitter's husband. I vaguely remember finally telling my parents. Nothing was ever really done because the babysitter was old and my parents didn't want to put her through a scandal.

I was sent back to the house with instructions to stay away from him. He didn't touch me again, but he was always there, watching. I was scared.

As an adult, I became a person I no longer recognized. My pain had become so great, it was easier to bury it in alcohol and pills than face it. One early morning, after a long night of drinking, I was so miserable that I took a handful of pills and decided I was done.

But God had other plans.

It was still more than a year before I surrendered and admitted that I was completely powerless over alcohol. Today I have more than two years of sobriety, am happily married to a wonderful man, and am so much closer in my walk with God. I know I fall short sometimes and life still gets me down, but life is good today and there is always something, no matter how small, to be grateful for. I am a strong woman today. I have my days, but today I can walk through the day without a pill or a drink . . . one day at a time. Today I choose life. Today I choose joy.

TERESA S.

In Memoriam

My childhood was a nightmare: sexual assault, physical abuse, abandonment. When I finally left home, I struggled to put it behind me. I wanted to forget it, so I did. Then I met the man who would become my husband. I was unaware he also had been abused—violated by a priest who was a family friend. He had told no one. His choice was also to forget. We were two damaged souls holding on to each other to find peace.

And for a while, it worked.

I didn't see the depression he struggled with. I should have noticed, should have helped. It was easy to deny his struggles when we were happy, especially when we were seeking our own escape. As my husband fought harder and harder to suppress his deepening depression, I refused to see us as anything but a happily married "normal" couple.

Finally it happened. He asked if he could lean on me. "But we'll both fall down," I responded. He couldn't need help. He was my beautiful, healthy, strong husband with arms that made me feel sheltered. Eventually he admitted he was having suicidal thoughts. I went into full protective mode as I dragged him to therapists, doctors, our priest, and finally had him admitted to a psychiatric hospital.

But the thing was, I never asked why. Perhaps I didn't want to know. Perhaps I was afraid of the answer. I was always great in a crisis, moving quickly into action, seeking help.

The hospital released him after two weeks, determining he no longer had thoughts of suicide. Everyone assured me he would never kill himself; he had so much to live for, such deep faith, such strong love. I wanted to believe them and so I brought him home. But I still never asked why.

We received a letter from the insurance company. Simply stated, they were denying further treatment because he was no longer a danger to himself or others. As we read the letter, which confirmed what I wanted to believe in black and white, he turned to me. With eyes betraying his exhaustion, he said, "I'm stuck." No, I assured him. If you ever need help, we will get it, no matter the cost. But again, I didn't ask him why—why he felt stuck, why he was feeling such pain.

I was only gone an hour. One hour. I later realized he had planned it, stealing my door key from my key ring. Hiding the spare we had secreted outside our front door.

He barricaded the house and hung himself in our garage.

Now I am left forever wondering about the answer to a question I never asked: Why?

SHANNON M.

When I began self-harming at twelve years old, I didn't really know what I was doing; I just knew that after I hurt myself, I felt a lot better. I was able to hide how I felt for quite some time. No one was aware of the extent of my problems until high school. I was an honor roll student with a lot of friends. I excelled at everything I did. I ran track and set school records, I played soccer on Division I teams, and I competed in dance competitions. On the outside, I seemed to have it all.

My junior year of high school I was hospitalized for the first time. I was diagnosed with bipolar disorder and put on medication.

After my hospital stay, I was able to find a great psychiatrist and therapist who really wanted to help me. Things seemed to be looking up for the first time in years. I went months without self-harming, which was something I had been unable to do since the self-harming began.

I have always struggled with my highs and lows, and cycled through relapses and recovery in my first year of college. But when I hit an all-time low my sophomore year, I didn't see a way out.

Friends of mine found me unconscious. They found my three-page note and the empty pill bottle. I was sent by ambulance to an emergency room where my stomach was pumped; I was in and out of consciousness for days. I don't remember a lot and, honestly, I think that's for the best. I was eventually sent home to a partial-hospitalization program.

Slowly I saw a light that got wider as time went on. Life got easier and I wasn't angry about being alive anymore. I wasn't just breathing, I was actually living—which is something I had not felt in almost a decade.

I haven't self-harmed in three years and I am currently working on my master's degree in social work. It may have taken a long time, but rock bottom became the solid foundation on which I rebuilt my life.

LISA D.

In Memoriam

Over Memorial Day weekend in 2012, my son Ian died by suicide. He was two weeks away from graduating high school.

Ian was everyone's big brother; his friends called him "the Rock." No one knew he suffered from depression. I knew that he was depressed to some degree, but his pain was deeper than I knew. We were very close, but his feelings toward his father were bottled up, making life very hard for him. Ian felt neglected by his father, and when he finally had communication with him, there were no apologies and no explanations.

Ian had always told me to be more adventurous, so I decided to skydive for my birthday. This was supposed to have been an adventure that Ian and I did together, but I wanted to breathe again and find a new normal that was comfortable for me.

I feel as if Ian passed a candle to me that I have to keep lit. I want to carry on doing what I think he would have done with his life: help others. I initiated a suicide prevention program for Ian's high school and I speak publicly about suicide prevention. I am celebrating Ian's life by traveling the world; it's my alternative therapy to help me live and enjoy life, even after suffering a heartbreaking loss.

REGINA P.

In Memoriam—for my alpha sister

My three sisters and I had an ongoing group chat, a constant exchange of chitchatting and inside jokes that was just one piece of the bond that made us so close. We talked about everything and nothing. The little things and the big things.

On September 6, 2014, everyone was chatting as usual. One of my sisters was scheduled to pick up her mother from the airport. She said good-bye as if it were any other "ttyl" type of good-bye.

But she never showed up at the airport. She wasn't answering her phone. We called the hospitals and police in her area, wondering if an accident had occurred. Her mother took a cab to her place, and there she saw the thing that would break each and every one of us into a thousand fragmented pieces. She found her, gone. Postmortem. Suicide by gunshot.

It is now coming up on two years and I don't have enough words to detail what all of us have been through in this time. On her birthday this year, I felt that it was my turn to join her. I was far too overwhelmed and felt like my expiration date had arrived. In the depth of that aggressive breakdown, I sent a text to my parents, a simple "I'm hurting, I need you." Very shortly thereafter, they were on the ten-hour drive to me.

I hadn't cleaned my apartment in days, weeks even. I slowly managed to pull myself out of the spot on my bed I had molded myself into and started straightening up. I was finally able to get off the merry-go-round of morbid decisions and plans. I felt relief flow through me when my parents arrived. What had started as my darkest day brightened; I felt my creative energy start to return after being dormant from grief. I knew it was my destiny to scale the mountains before me, no matter how high or impossible they seem.

All I can do is the best I can.

AMIE R.

I was fourteen years old, two months away from graduating eighth grade and excited about the prospect of entering high school, when I was diagnosed with minimal change kidney disease. A year and a half of hospitals, medicine, and kidney biopsies ensued. I went into remission once, but soon the disease came back with a vengeance. The second biopsy showed a shadow over my kidney that was caused by something unknown. As a result, I was put on oral chemotherapy and prednisone. The medicines basically broke down my skin cells and, with the dramatic weight gain and loss associated with the disease, I now have stretch marks over 80 to 85 percent of my body. Arms, back, stomach, legs, feet—basically everywhere. I would joke with my mom that I lost my looks before I even got them. My humor helped me through some of the roughest patches of this experience, but then humor stopped working.

One night I took a paper clip to my arm. I succeeded in scratching up my arm terribly before I went crying to my mother. We went to the doctor, who told me that she had expected to see me about this issue six months ago. I was diagnosed with depression, put on medication, and that was that. The medication did what it was supposed to do, and I never gave my depression a second thought.

Then 2014 rolled around. I was twenty-eight years old and had been living with my depression for thirteen years. I was working in a pretty toxic environment that was both mentally and emotionally taxing, and in March, I lost both of my grandmothers within seventeen hours of each other. That was kind of the beginning of the end. It started with little things: I stopped putting in my contacts, then I stopped putting on makeup, then any effort into my appearance went out the window.

Then I broke.

I went on a leave of absence from work, started taking new medication, and started to see a therapist. I also went back home to Minnesota. I visited my grandmother's grave for the first time since her funeral and I cried. And I cried and I cried. It was very healing.

I did finally return to work. My first day back I received so much love from my friends that it was overwhelming. In a conversation with a friend of mine I mentioned my depression and he looked at me and said, "You have depression?" like it was this great big shock. And, I guess, to those who are not that close to me, it would be a surprise. I am an insanely happy person. I'm constantly joking around and having fun. Good luck trying to get me to be serious for more than five minutes. You would never guess that I have depression, but I don't advertise it, either. My pain is on the inside. This goes to show that you can never judge someone, because you don't know what battle they are fighting on the inside.

I know there are days when waking up and living is a struggle, but I choose to continue that fight. Life is worth living.

SAMANTHA F.

I was molested and abused by family members starting when I was really young. I kept it to myself, but it ate away at me. When I was a teenager, a close friend's dad destroyed me. He took all my self-worth. I was in and out of hospitals after that. I wanted to die, and failed at every attempt. I was diagnosed bipolar and placed on several different medications until, eventually, my mom gave me up. I spent a few years in and out of foster homes and group homes. I would self-harm to deal with the pain, until I found drugs. It wasn't long before I was homeless and on the streets, addicted to drugs and selling my body to get them.

I have been through the depths of hell. It took me a long time to realize my self-worth again, and I'm still learning to love myself. My goal in life now is to help people who are struggling. To let them know they're not alone. I continue to live life one day at a time, sometimes one moment at a time. We can survive. No matter what our pasts were, we don't have to go on like that anymore.

AMY O.

A blood clot caused my stomach to literally explode when I was eighteen, leaving me in a coma for months. What I learned after I was readmitted, reconstructed, reoperated on, and "fixed up" several times is that no surgery is a guarantee. Without a stomach, it was six years of often not being able to eat or drink. Every time I'd have a medical setback, doctors would advise me to just "stop eating and drinking for now." I would be put back on IVs and have to switch to "machine mode." Food was suddenly declared a fatal danger, and now intravenous nutrition was the only way to save my system. As the obedient patient, I complied with my doctors' orders for several years. It was an odd mix of staying numb, isolated, and distracted while enduring twenty-seven surgeries over the course of a decade.

Being numb to my circumstances was the easiest way to deal with them, and I locked myself in my room for hours at a time. When I became desperate to feel, I would cook for my family in an attempt to experience the human sensations of hunger without actually feeding myself. I could smell my minestrone soup simmering and feel the flour work its way into the pizza dough. Both allowed me to feel alive in the small ways that were available to me. I either felt numb or painfully sad, and there didn't seem to be an opportunity for any new feelings to grow. If I wasn't numb, I'd start crying, get anxious and tense, and immediately think back to my surgeries, to my life before surgery, and feel the hatred for the path my life had taken.

But part of feeling human is being angry, frustrated, worried, and anxious about circumstances beyond our control. Part of feeling human is becoming overwhelmed with the agonizing question "Why me?" as we shake our fists at the sky, wondering how life can be so unfair.

One morning, I woke up with an anger that was so overwhelming, the energy of it frightened me. I didn't know what to do; the emotions were overpowering. My thoughts and feelings threatened to swallow me whole.

With no rational thought in my head, I ran out the door and started running without knowing where I was going. It was the adrenaline of panic; I felt unsafe in my situation and wanted to run far away from it. I had never felt an energy like that before, a red-hot high moving through my legs and tingling in my chest before eventually falling from my eyes in tears I hoped would dry in the whipping wind on my face.

I kept running as far away from my life as I could. I was too scared to kill myself, and I didn't think I wanted to, either. I wanted a middle ground, wanted to exist in another world—and if I ran long enough, I'd get there somehow.

I ran for three hours before I found a highway and, without thinking, I started running onto the shoulder of it. I thought, *The farther I go, the farther this will all be behind me.* Of course, on the day I decide to run for my life, it starts to rain . . . and thunder. Suddenly, the highway was flooded, I was drenched, and I had cars beeping at me, wondering what a frail little girl in a T-shirt was doing running on the shoulder of the highway.

It was only a matter of time before a police car pulled up to me and asked me to get inside. I was shaking, angry, confused, embarrassed, and nervous—like I had just gotten a detention in school. The officer said, "I've gotten about thirty calls in the past twenty minutes saying this eighty-pound girl is running on the shoulder of the highway. Where did you think you were going?"

I was upset that my escape had been halted, and suddenly very ashamed. Wiping away tears, I stammered, "To the mall."

"You thought you could get to the mall on the shoulder of the highway?"

"Yes."

From the front seat, he turned around and looked at me to say, "I can drive you to the mall."

I refused to look at him, pressed my elbows into my sides, and barely whispered, "No, I'll go home."

He called my worried parents to tell them I was okay. My mother, after recovering from her concerned rage, asked me what on earth I thought I was doing. I told her simply that I was trying to escape. I was frustrated with my body and I couldn't take living under these circumstances for an indefinite amount of time. All she said was, "But you took your body with you."

I didn't want to kill myself because, in my heart, I knew how much I adored life. But I needed a break. I wanted life to get easier. I was sick of living in fear. Then I realized it wasn't feeling happy I was chasing, it was feeling alive. I just wanted to feel connected.

Life may leave me winded, angry, frustrated, panicked, or overwhelmed with sadness, but it's the rush of being alive. And I'm so glad I stayed on track.

RUBY M.

The first time I cut myself was with a pair of (to my frustration) blunt scissors that didn't really get me anywhere.

The next time was with a razor blade. *That* got me somewhere. I still have the scars on my ankles and thighs today, almost eight years later.

When I was sixteen, I fell in love with my best friend, who was closer to me than a sister. For the sake of the story let's call her Jane. It messed me up; I had all these thoughts spiraling through my head. . . .

I . . . I can't be . . .

My family is very religious, and so are many of my friends. I was forced to keep my feelings a secret because I thought it was evil and wrong.

I . . . can't be . . . gay . . . ?

Jane would tell me about all the things she did with boys, and as a result I began to punish myself for envying those boys. I wished I could be the one to kiss her, wished I could hold her close to me . . . and I wished I didn't feel the way I did.

The cuts I punished myself with inched ever closer to the veins on my wrists and even my hands. In hindsight, I suppose it was a subconscious way of crying for help, hoping that someone would notice the scars and ask me if I was okay. No one did, of course. Not until my secret got out.

I couldn't hide it anymore. I confessed to a classmate that I was in love with my best friend. I honestly thought that classmate was going to keep my secret.

She didn't.

I eventually told Jane how I felt and she told me she loved me but not in that way. As people started to see through my indifferent charade and began to suspect that I was gay, they dropped me like I meant nothing to them. To top it off, my family was in a financial rut and we were struggling to pay school fees, which added more pressure to an already tense situation.

I hit rock bottom. I was at a family function but was determined to end my pain. I ripped off my angel-wing necklace and attempted to slice my veins open. I didn't get very far. I gave up and decided to drink my sorrows away. I wound up on the floor at the entrance to the venue curled up in a fetal position, crying out in pain. I felt everyone I'd loved had betrayed me.

After that night my mom sent me to the psychologist every week. I began to open up to my family again and my mom told me she always knew about my feelings. She said that mothers know things. She told me it was okay and that she would always love me no matter what.

Jane and I slowly became strangers and, as I felt it happening, I felt more and more helpless . . . I was holding on so tightly to someone who was already gone. I stopped eating and developed insomnia. I felt like I'd be happier if I was dead.

I remember staring at the blue walls in my room and hearing a voice inside my head. I obeyed his command and gripped the closest thing to a rope I had—a piece of denim material—and wrapped it around my neck. I felt the oxygen leaving me, and for the first time in a long time I felt euphoric! I felt like I was soaring, flying away from this wreck of an existence. But it was over all too soon as I fell to the ground, coughing uncontrollably. I inhaled a sliver of air and choked on it. As I lay on the ground losing consciousness, I told myself it would be over soon . . . I would be gone. But I woke up hours later. I kept the event to myself; I never told a soul.

Because of all the anxiety and panic attacks, I developed pseudo-seizures. I have been in and out of the hospital since last November, and the doctors say the seizures are a delayed reaction from hiding my emotions for years.

Amid all the turmoil, I met my boyfriend. Yes, you read that right: boyfriend. He showed me that for me, love isn't about genitalia but about the person on the inside. No matter how cliché it sounds, he has saved me from myself.

The best part is: I don't want to die anymore. I realize now that my family will accept me no matter who or what I am or what I do. I have incredible friends now, ones who care about me and are happy for my happiness just as I am for theirs. Life is getting better and I am getting stronger. I know what it means, at last, to be truly loved.

Megan S.

Molly F.

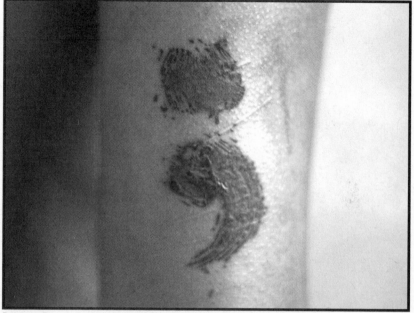

Raianna P.

Rosa G.

NICOLÁS R.

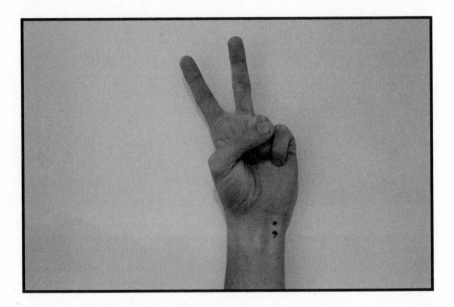

The hardest things I have lived with—that I still continue to live with—are addiction and depression. These challenges cycle around and enable each other, and took me to the point where I didn't think life was worth living anymore. I think about those moments when I promised myself I would not take that hit and I did it anyway, and it hurts deep in my soul. Finding the strength to distance myself from the drug that entrapped me in its claws meant leaving behind my first love, my friendships, and everything that had given me purpose for so long. It's been a constant struggle against the current. I've shed a sea of tears, and even my screams do not express the immense pain I have felt.

Across this arduous journey toward a better life, I reencountered my true self. I have found a version of myself that is brave, unstoppable, and conscious. I realized that no one will take care of this problem; I must always take the first step, loving and taking care of myself. I will live to experience different loves and friendships, but the only common factor throughout my life will be me. I decided to create a me that I can feel proud about, regardless of my surroundings. The best part is that I can see glimpses of this person and I am blessed to say that I know how I am supposed to deal with life from now on, to ensure this happy me in the future.

I have learned from my suffering that I am my priority, and I must value myself over anything, situation or person. This way I will be able to say that I have myself, someone whom I love, even in the most difficult times.

HAYLEIGH H.

In Memoriam

Four weeks ago, part of me died along with my brother, Ben. We had only just lost Mum nineteen months earlier. What else did life think we could possibly handle?

And yet, who would be so lucky to watch a movie with their brother right before he passed? Who would be so lucky that their final words to their brother were "I love you"?

Ben left the house that night and seemed totally normal. He told me he was going around to his best mate's house for a chat. About twenty minutes later, I received a call from my brother's partner, asking if I knew where Ben went. He had called her to say his good-byes and told her he was in "the middle of nowhere." I rang around to my siblings and Dad to get the word out quickly.

My whole family raced to Ben's location, which we'd found using an app on his phone. We all expected to find him crying in his car. That's the kind of sensitive soul he was.

We discovered that Ben had intentionally driven his car into a tree, very close to the farm where we'd grown up. He was killed instantly.

The warm, innocent, caring boy who helped bind us all together was suddenly gone.

Ben was twenty-two years old.

Ben was employed full-time.

Ben loved his boss and job.

Ben had three loving sisters.

Ben's family were all very close.

Ben had enough savings for a house deposit.

Ben had a beautiful baby daughter.

Ben was waiting for his brand-new car to arrive.

Ben only drank occasionally.

Ben wasn't involved in drugs.

Ben was always happy.

Or so it seemed.

There were no signs.

No warnings.

No note.

I tell Ben's story to help people understand that it's okay not to be okay. There is help, and hope.

RICHARD B.

Standing in the darkened library of memories, moonlight shines through the window as my mind starts reflecting back on my journey through schizophrenia. I open a leather-bound book and watch as a projection of a memory floats out of the pages. I can see myself sitting in a cabin in Mount Gambier, South Australia. I was alone and homeless. Even now I start to hear the hallucinations I heard back then, voices of persecution yelling at me from outside the windows.

It was a time when nothing made sense. I did not know I had schizophrenia.

Snapping the book shut, I place it back on the shelf, take a deep breath, and steady myself after the intensity of the memory. I sit heavily on the couch underneath the window of the library, my eyes tired.

Soon after my arrival in Mount Gambier, I started on medication and came under the care of some doctors; I managed to secure a private rental and worked as a laborer in a vineyard in Coonawarra. I can see fresh dew droplets on the baby vine leaves heralding spring, smell the aroma of heavy fruits infused with independence and freedom.

I didn't give up in my darkest moment, and ended up finding the light that infuses my life to this day. In the library of memories, I hear birdsong welcoming the dawn outside the window.

BEATRIX B.

I was fourteen when I started to self-harm. A few cat scratches that I wouldn't allow to heal became the start of a decade of addiction. In the beginning, it was nothing I couldn't pass off as accidents or just being clumsy. But it soon escalated. Eventually it became part of my daily routine, waking up early before school to clean myself up from the night before and redress my bandaged arms. Anything to avoid people finding out my secret obsession.

By the age of fifteen it was difficult for me to go a day without self-harm. Added onto this was my eating disorder, as well as my exhausting obsessive-compulsive disorder. It was just a matter of time before somebody noticed, and someone at school did; I was quickly referred to my local child and adolescent mental health team, who began trying to help me. After many battles, some progress, and further relapse, it was decided that I would benefit from inpatient care. I spent almost a year in inpatient services, and further time in outpatient services. Intensive therapy helped me to understand my emotions and taught me to deal with them in positive ways. I owe my life to those professionals who helped me to become well enough to return to school to complete my education.

Despite two relapses in my mental health, I have managed to be well enough to apply for and attend university. When I look back to the angry teenager I was, intent on ending her life and adamant that life was always going to be the same, I wish I could go back and show her the future. The reality is that actually, the future is bright and exciting, full of ups and downs, but on the whole, life is good.

MICHELLE S.

Semicolon bipolar awareness butterfly

A couple years ago, I ended up getting admitted to a mental hospital for suicidal ideation due to lots of bullying online. I honestly loved it there, but I missed being home with my husband and dogs. After I was released from the hospital, I relapsed at least two more times, and was diagnosed with bipolar disorder. It took me a while to accept that I needed medication and to not feel ashamed of taking it, but now I'm on the road to recovery.

I've had one crazy life, but I've learned it's true: "This too shall pass."

ASHLEY K.

My name is Ashley. I am eighteen years old, and I am holding strong. I take one day at a time. I mostly lean on myself, and I have several mantras that help. I recently had one of them tattooed on my forearm: *alis volat propriis*, which means "she flies with her own wings." I know that I can't depend too much on others for my happiness because I won't end up being happy. That's not the way life works.

My story is not over. Yours isn't, either.

ROCHELLE T.

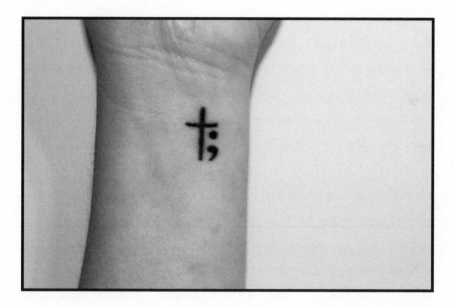

In the brutal beauty of hindsight, I can now see that I was living through the early stages of an abusive relationship when my first daughter was born. But when he left us two and a half years later, I didn't feel free. Instead I fell into a very deep pit of depression. I was completely numb and did not want to live. But my loving, supportive family made sure I got the helped I needed.

Despite this, the belief that I was a failure as a mother grew and I began to self-harm. I justified this by telling myself I deserved it because I had failed my daughter. Each time I believed I had let her down—if I yelled at her, put her in her room for time out, wasn't there when she wanted me, sent her off to spend time with her dad—whatever it was, I would go upstairs, lock myself in the storeroom, and put cuts into my wrists. I remember one occasion of actually scratching the word *failure* into my arm. I wanted it to hurt because I believed I had hurt her and should be punished.

With medication, counseling, my amazing family, and my faith, I began to rebuild my life and recognize I had purpose; I knew I had to keep going for my daughter. I finished university and got a teaching degree, and no longer needed to take antidepressants.

Then I reconciled with my husband. With that bitingly, beautifully clear hindsight, I can see I did that out of fear. I also had an unrealistic fairy-tale mentality, and a desire to give my daughter a stereotypical family. Returning to a manipulative, controlling, and abusive environment caused my mental health to decline. Slowly but surely I lost my self-worth, cried constantly, and didn't want to be around people anymore. I was isolated from my family and struggled to parent my daughter, who had also become a victim of his abuse. I started to self-harm worse than ever and needed medication again.

A couple of years later, when I got a permanent full-time job, I mustered the courage to leave and step out on my own. Within a week, I discovered I was pregnant. This was a game changer; I stayed with my husband. I went off my medication for the duration of my pregnancy and after the birth of my second daughter had severe postpartum depression, suffering intense feelings of guilt and failure. I did not waste time getting on antidepressants and beginning counseling, but my husband's abusiveness only intensified.

That is, until the day when he committed the worst abuse I had witnessed from him, toward our twelve-year-old daughter. I was now five months pregnant with our third daughter, and after he physically hurt me, too, I asked myself, *What am I teaching my girls? How can I stand by, just tolerating this and allowing it to happen to them, to us?* So I left and again found myself living with Mum and Dad. Being pregnant, I was not on antidepressants but was closely monitored and, after giving birth, I left the hospital, back on my medication. Things were different this time around, though, as I almost lost my life giving birth to her and this gave me a whole new perspective on living.

Since finally breaking free of more than a decade of abuse (physical, financial, mental, emotional, and spiritual), I still live with mild depression. I have been through some rough teenage years with my eldest daughter, helping her cope with and begin to heal from all the trauma she experienced. Having been there myself, I was better equipped to understand and support her.

I carry on in this life because I have HOPE. I have hope because I had people who never gave up on me, and I developed a faith in God that showed me my life has purpose.

HANNAH E.

White walls, smell of strong medicines, eerie feeling; everything is a blur. I can't really remember what happened to me the night my parents found me almost lifeless on my bed. It wasn't really my intention to die that day. All I wanted was relief from the pain I'd been going through for years.

Even before my diagnosis of major depressive disorder and borderline personality disorder five years ago, I knew something wasn't right. There were voices in my head saying "You will never be enough." To get through each day, I turned to vices: alcohol, drugs, and non-stop partying. I was too proud to admit to myself that I needed help, let alone admit it to others. All I could think about was how I could make the pain go away. I became obsessed with pleasing everyone around me. I craved acceptance. I begged for love and approval. I felt so alone, miserable, and incomplete.

One particular night, I was so tired from everything. I'd been awake for forty-eight hours. All I wanted was to go to sleep and leave everything behind for a while. I popped my sleeping pills and washed them down with beer. It didn't do a thing. So I popped another batch, again and again until I consumed it all. I blacked out.

It was dark and eerie. I was startled by a ring from my cell phone. It was my friend calling. I was not feeling so well but I picked up anyway. My friend was asking me what was wrong because I sounded different. I told him I felt sick and couldn't breathe.

"I did something wrong. Help me. I am sorry. I don't want to die . . ." Those are the last words I remember saying.

Immediately after that incident, I finally admitted to myself that I needed to seek professional help. I've since gone through psychotherapy, developed a strong support group, and relearned to love myself more.

My demons are still with me. But I know now how to handle them. I am stronger and wiser, and I know now how to love and value myself.

JOE D.

I've been struggling with depression since my diagnosis at fourteen. I'm thankful every day that I chose to press on, because now I study music in college and do what I love every single day. Music gives me a way to express myself where words fail me.

RICHARD E.

My father, a Vietnam veteran, committed suicide due to PTSD. Still, I followed in his footsteps and joined the US Army. As a combat medic in Afghanistan, I saw everything from amputations to death. Transitioning back to civilian life after my tour was difficult; I turned to alcohol as a treatment to suppress the demons within. I was also plagued with insomnia and attention deficit issues.

November 2015 marked twenty years since my father's passing. Depression hit me hard. My grades dropped, I secluded myself from my social circle, and I truly felt alone. Near the end of November, something inside me was fighting to get out. I sought a helping hand

and got the support I needed, but I was hit again with depression and PTSD symptoms earlier this year. My friend and Special Operations member Matt McClintock passed away due to wounds suffered while fighting in Afghanistan. I was reminded of the death, wounds, and all the burials I'd seen in my life. I drank.

By the start of spring semester at college, I'd had enough of just simply dealing with the issues. A Women and Gender Studies class taught me to "claim my education," and I started becoming more passionate about suicide and PTSD awareness. Veterans and civilians both need to know it's okay to get the mental health care you need. There's nothing wrong with asking for help.

LAUREN K.

No one wants to talk about it, even though it's common and affects so many people. "Shh. Don't talk about that, Lauren. People will think you're crazy."

So there's this thing called a chemical imbalance in the brain. Maybe you've heard about it? Apparently, it's science.

Let's face it: No matter what you say, certain people will always attach a stigma to mental illness. You have a heart attack? You're covered. Insurance covers you. Your family and friends send you balloons and flowers and "Hey, get well soon."

I mean, that's great. People should care.

But you have depression? Maybe you're suicidal?

You get strange glances, awkward responses, and uncomfortable remarks. I get it. It's a prickly subject. No one wants to talk about it.

But when people say things like "But you have so much going for you! How in the world can you be so depressed?!" that implies many things. It implies my depression makes you uncomfortable. It implies you think you don't understand me, or you think we're so different from each other. It implies you think I'm kind of ungrateful, or there's something wrong with my worldview. It implies you're unsure if we can be friends, because you don't know how to act around me and my "disease."

I get it. Someone who has never experienced depression (especially severe, suicidal depression) might not easily understand these things. And of course, people who love you mean well. But none of these implied messages make a depressed person feel any better. How could they?

I've been severely depressed. I've been suicidal. I've done stupid things. What needs to change is the health-care system and the attitudes people have about mental health. Where now we have stigmas, we need support.

But what do I know? I'm just a girl with depression. Trying to navigate through life, just like everyone else. Maybe sometimes, for me and people like me, it's just a little bit harder.

Depression isn't weakness. It's an illness. Have compassion for people, no matter what they're going through. As they say, you haven't walked a mile in their shoes.

JAMIE B.

I have been battling social anxiety and depression since I was a child. I had a very hard time in school, especially in high school. Halfway through my ninth-grade year, I became overwhelmed with anxiety and became severely depressed. I was homebound. People didn't understand social anxiety, even though some—like my family—tried. I felt so alone, anxiety suffocating me. I couldn't go anywhere by myself for fear of having to talk to someone. I couldn't order food in a restaurant. When I was out and saw someone I knew who might talk to me, I would avoid them the best I could. I felt like something was wrong with me, like I was a freak.

As I have gotten older, I have realized I am special. I was put here for a reason. I have learned to love myself. This makes dealing with everything easier. I realized I have something to offer the world. I still struggle with social anxiety and depression today, but I just know my life is much more important than I thought it was in the past.

Sometimes I still feel like I can't go on, but I have two beautiful girls who look at me as their role model. If I don't love myself, how will my girls know how to love themselves? They are both aware of the struggles I go through. I don't hide it from them. Together as a family, we take it one day at a time.

KEVIN S.

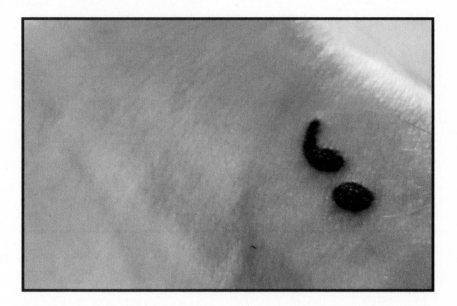

Sometimes, I feel like a dung beetle. (I know, but hear me out.)

What starts off as the tiniest piece of crap gets rolled around in my mind until it's the biggest load of bullshit ever. Sometimes, this bullshit accidentally rolls over other people and ruins relationships, but mostly, it stops me from being able to see my way forward.

Right now I am doing okay. I have people who make me drop that load and, occasionally, I am lucky enough to see it crumble and disappear. Other times, they just help by reminding me that I can simply roll it off a cliff without having to follow it.

It's okay not to be okay, as long as we keep rolling.

RUXANDRA B.

My whole life I was heavier than most kids. I developed faster than the other girls. I was simply . . . different. And I can honestly say it was not my doing. I was never a fast-food junkie, and I didn't spend my time eating sweets or snacks. But still . . . I was different. *So what?* one might ask. *Everyone is different in one way or another.*

Have you ever been called names?

Have you ever been laughed at, mocked, bullied to the point where you don't have any tears left to cry?

I have.

I was a child. A child just like them. I didn't get it. I didn't understand why they laughed, why they didn't talk to me, why they called me all those names. Whale, fat, fatty . . . you name it, I've heard it. I heard it all. And somewhere in the back of my head, in the dark depths of my heart, to this day I still hear those mean words. And it hurt so much back then. It still does sometimes. Like a thousand knives jammed in my heart, in my gut. I cried . . . oh how much I cried. Every single day. For years and years. No child deserves to cry like that. No other human being deserves to feel like that.

I despised mornings. Because I had to go to school, and the kids were mean to me. It seemed like they hated me simply because I was different. And I hated them because I felt so unwanted. I was also afraid. Afraid of the words, those words that hurt more than anything I've ever experienced, even to this day. Afraid of their faces laughing at me. Afraid of crying time and time again, knowing that nobody believed how mean the kids were to me.

I spent so many nights crying myself to sleep because I'd have to go back to hell again in the morning, I lost count. I can't remember how many times I wished I could fall asleep and never wake up. I wondered how much it would hurt to cut my wrists and die, or if jumping from my window, a balcony, a bridge would do the trick.

My message to everyone out there? The laughs, the mean words . . . they hurt. They sting. They burn. And they can kill. They can change someone forever. They can give you scars that will never fully heal. They can make you wish you had never been born. They are evil, unnecessary stabs in the back, free tickets to hell.

Please think twice. You don't know the stories behind us. You don't know, yet you make us victims for your amusement. Don't be the bully who says the one word that fills up the glass and makes it tip over, pushing a person to take their own life.

I want this to be a story of how inner strength can pull you back into the light even when you are thrown into the deepest darkness. It's been more than a decade since I was that tortured little girl, but somewhere inside me, she's there still—sobbing, asking God to take her with Him. It is still hard for me to be strong every day. Once you've felt hell, it will always linger there inside.

Stay strong. The fight is yours to win.

MARCIA D.

When I was younger I went through a lot of pain. To describe that pain to someone who has never been through it is very difficult, but it's the kind of pain that can pull you inside of yourself so far that you lose yourself in it. Sometimes it hurt so much inside that there was no way to show this deep emotional burden.

So I would cut my arm.

I would cut when I was overwhelmed by this deep pain and then put a Band-Aid on it and nurse it until it was better. The wound was a reminder to me that I was in pain, but that I could heal. My scars reminded me that I went through something horrible, but I made it through. I struggled most of my life in such pain and grief and wondered when I was going to heal. Through therapy, medication, and a strong relationship with God, my boyfriend, and our three beautiful daughters, I have found more and more reasons to fight.

Even though we go through deep emotional pain through our lives, it doesn't mean we cannot move forward, live longer, and embrace the pain to allow God to make it beautiful. God has been with me my whole life. He was there when I cut and He is with me still.

LACEY B.

When my depression started, it seemed to be the product of many things happening all at once: I had a new job, I was learning to drive (which I disliked immensely), I was saddled with a very difficult college course load, and I had to cope with the loss of a beloved relative. Even now, looking back, it seems like a lot. At the time, it felt like an impossible weight to bear.

I became very distant, I would cry for no apparent reason (which was very unlike me), and I started finding it hard to explain how I felt. Talking also became a big issue; I just couldn't form conversation. My mum took me down to the doctors' three times in one week, and each time they dismissed my symptoms as stress. I could not understand what was happening to me. My life and my emotions felt as if they were going on a downward spiral—a spiral totally out of my control.

Things soon worsened dramatically. I could not speak, I lost all my concentration, I could not watch TV or read books. I couldn't shower or feed myself. I was virtually incapacitated. I had frequent panic attacks if I tried to leave the house. I also felt so incredibly lonely, deep down into my soul. Some mornings, I would refuse to get out of bed; I felt as if I had nothing to live for. All the days rolled into one and every night I would hope that the next day would be better. It never was.

I just wanted to die. I would go online and research ways to die. I would beg my mum to kill me. I would beat myself up every single day, telling myself I was useless, worthless, a waste of space. I would throw myself down stairs to feel pain. I would also pinch the backs of my legs until they became horribly bruised and painful. I lost all of my self-confidence and would tell myself that I was extremely ugly, and that no one would ever like me because of this.

As I was unable to look after myself, my mum took on all of my care. I was totally dependent on her to live. When my doctor realized I was seriously ill, I was referred to the children's and adolescent mental health services nearby. In the eight months it took for my medication to make a difference, I lost nearly all my friends. No one understood what was happening to me. I felt as if my life was over, as if I couldn't ever be a normal teenager again.

Stupidly, I stopped taking my medicine without any supervision from my doctor. Back down into the spiral of darkness I went. It was harder to pull myself out this time, but not as hard as it would be a year later, when it happened again. That third time, the depression and anxiety developed into psychosis. My brain didn't feel like my own; I thought I was being controlled, thought things that weren't true. I heard voices that weren't there, thought everyone was talking about me and saying horrible things. I even saw things that weren't there. It felt as though I was living in another world that was twisted and cruel. I thought my own family was lying to me. It was such a confusing, dark time.

I've only recently recovered from this, and I still don't understand it. All I know is that I'm feeling a lot better and am finally starting to rebuild my life again. I have a lovely boyfriend and an amazing family who were and always will be right by my side, supporting me through whatever happens. I also see my psychosis recovery worker once a week, and that's really helping me gain my confidence back.

Depression is not just feeling down or sad; it is a nasty, controlling illness that can take hold of every aspect in your life. There is a way out eventually. It may be a long and tiring journey, but you will get there!

KRISTIE C.

In Memoriam

There is no time limit on grief. You don't wake up one day and decide "Well, I'm done grieving now." Time moves on and new days come. The pain lives in you, and you just learn to live with it. I've been learning for twenty years.

He was the cutest guy I'd ever seen. Dark hair, dark eyes, tan skin, and a killer smile. He was well liked, could charm most anyone, and teachers adored him. Yet he was also one of the "bad boys," and I was one of the "good girls." Our relationship was short-lived, but what came of it was a bouncing nine-pound, three-ounce baby boy; I was just fourteen years old at the time and he was sixteen. We broke up shortly after I got pregnant and didn't speak for months. I went to California to spend my summer with my dad, and that must have been when my son's father started his journey to a much darker place.

Back at school in the fall, I was called to the guidance counselor's office. She sat me down and told me that he had been shot. My immediate reaction was to ask if he was okay. With tears in her eyes and a broken heart of her own for a lost student, she told me no, he had died.

My version of the world shattered and became gloomy for a very long time. Our son was just shy of nine months old; they had never met. His story didn't have to end. And in some ways it didn't, as it continues to live on through his son and me every day. We will always miss him and think of him daily. That part of the grieving process will never stop. How do we find hope? We talk about it with others. We share our story, his story. We have a support system and we try to educate others. No one is ever alone. There are perfect strangers who really do care about you and the things you are dealing with. Help is out there. Hope carries on.

LINE F.

One of the therapists I spoke to gave me this very strange thing to think of when I was down: "When you feel sad," she said, "think of your feet." It took me a while to understand why I was supposed to think of something so stupid as my feet, but eventually I realized it was because the concept was so strange, it left a smile on my face every time.

Rhian L.

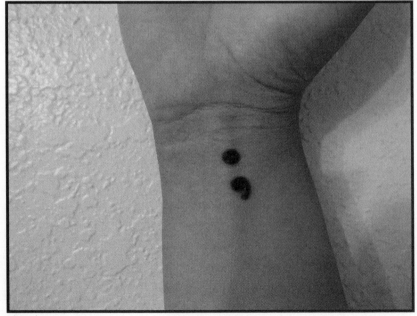

Alquidamia A.

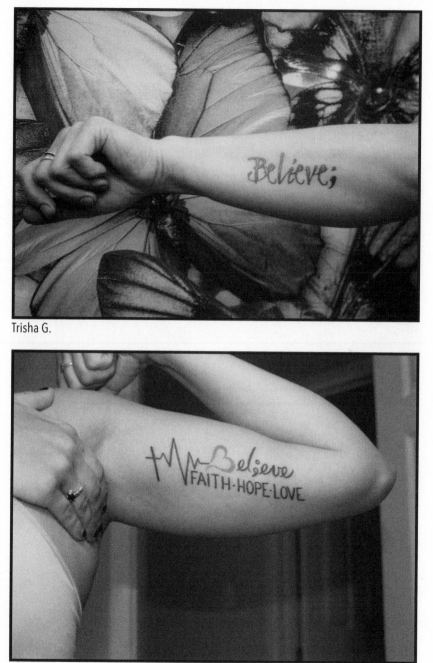

Trisha G.

Victoria K.

EMILY R.

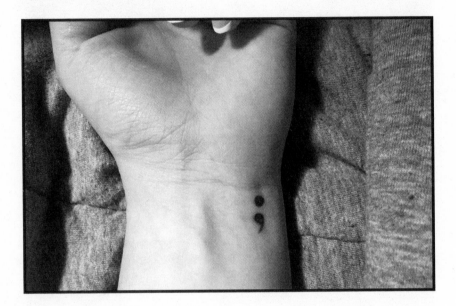

When I was a sophomore in high school, I felt depressed even though I didn't have a reason to. I had many trustworthy friends, and a loving family surrounded me. But something inside made me hate myself. I felt hopeless and nothing shook the feeling I had. I hated the way my body looked, which soon led to an eating disorder and occasional cutting. I just kept hearing a voice in my head saying that I wasn't good enough and that I needed to be a certain weight in order to be considered beautiful. I was terrified to eat anything because calories led to pounds and pounds led to that voice in my head. I never told anyone how I felt until I got to the point where I am now, a freshman in college.

One day, while sitting in my college dorm, feeling at my lowest, I came across Project Semicolon. I loved the whole meaning of the semicolon. I would draw the symbol on the same exact spot on my arm every day as a reminder that my story is continuing.

Soon, I started to feel more comfortable talking about my feelings. I wrote a paper for my English class about body image that told my story and the things I went through to fit society's false idea of "perfection." When I got my graded paper back, my professor wrote to me saying how she had suffered from an eating disorder when she was around my age, and she told me how she overcame it and became stronger. We started to really bond over the topic, which gave me more confidence to talk to people about it.

This is only the beginning, but I've been clean for two months. I am not my mistakes and I'm proud to say that I am happy with the person I am. That's something I haven't said in years.

JESSAMYN S.

The summer before I started high school was full of heartbreak. I had grown up pretending to be someone I wasn't, denying that the way a girl's hand felt in mine was perfection to me. I was convinced my father would not approve of having a lesbian daughter. This was, I would learn, only one way my heart could be broken.

On a hot summer day in August, I was babysitting two sweet little boys. While I prepped them for their nap, a stranger walked right into the home and gestured for me to send the boys away. He pulled up his shirt a bit to show me he had a .38-caliber pistol. I secured the boys in their room and went back out into the living room, where the guy assaulted me. He then made me take a shower and watched me wash myself. From there on out I was on a path of self-destruction. Drugs, alcohol, depression . . . I barely graduated high school. More than once I have contemplated suicide. I have been on multiple meds, from Prozac to Wellbutrin, Celexa to lithium.

Things got bad, but then they got better. I have a beautiful life and am surrounded by wonderful people. I remind myself I am worth this life, this love. I spread the word, the love; I talk to people, I let people around me know I am here for them. They are not alone. And neither are you.

HEATHER L.

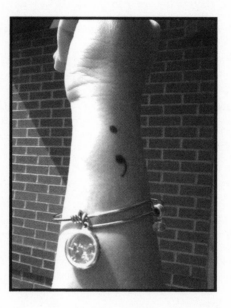

My father committed suicide when I was eight. Nature or nurture? I learned that depression and anxiety can be genetic. Sometimes the feeling inside is so overwhelming that the only thing that helps is to squeeze so hard that my nails dig into my skin. I had an "episode" once around friends and couldn't look at them for days afterward. It was like they had seen me naked; I was so embarrassed.

When my daughter was diagnosed with anxiety disorder and OCD, I thought, *Great, I've passed it on and kept the genetic flaw flowing. I'm broken and now I've broken her too.* As it turned out, she was my greatest blessing. She caused me to identify my anxieties. She helped me talk about it. She helped me gain strength and bring my secrets out of the closet. By talking about anxiety and advocating for her and her needs, I grew stronger.

My daughter just comes out and says to others, "I have anxiety." She has stopped the cycle—no more hiding. We wear our anxiety like a badge of honor. It makes us emotional and sensitive and caring all at the same time.

She thinks I am the one helping her, but little does she know—she's helping me, too.

JESSICA B.

Obsessions. Counting rituals. Irrational fears of glass ketchup bottles and bars of soap. Always covering my hands with sweatshirt sleeves to avoid germs and contamination. Staring at digital clocks, adding, subtracting, and multiplying the numbers. Doing the same with license plates. I was too young at twelve years old to know what was happening, so it continued.

Despite the challenges of OCD, I found help and support. I graduated high school and college. I even found work as a preschool teacher.

Then I hit a wall. Obsessive-compulsive disorder took over my life. I was having intrusive thoughts, health anxiety, and fears of catching illnesses and diseases. I was still plagued by irrational fears of ketchup, sharks, and soap. Medication after medication, therapy after therapy—nothing changed. I moved to a residential OCD unit, where I faced my fears, did exposure therapy, wrote my intrusive thoughts on paper, used bars of soap, and made great progress through great effort. I even used two empty glass ketchup bottles in an art project; I decorated them, added googly eyes, named them, and gave them personalities.

While I kept going to sessions and trying to stay positive, things slowly began to unravel. My obsessions and rituals took over, depression and anxiety crept in, and I decided to go back to the residential unit to treat my symptoms further, and address the bulimia I had developed. Slowly but surely, I made progress.

Now I am taking one day at a time, moment by moment. There are ups and downs, but I am working hard to stay strong and move along. I am living my life according to my values and trying to share my story of struggle and strength, as there is a light at the end of the tunnel, and a glimpse of hope.

ANDREAS H.

Thinking about my bipolar diagnosis and my past, I remember bouts of mania and depression when I was younger; teachers thought I was wired on drugs when I was just having a manic episode, or people thought I was stoned when my depression was rearing its ugly head. It wasn't until years later that I would find myself curled up in a closet, not wanting to go to work, crying my eyes out, hiding from the world. I realized I needed help.

Even today, as I battle various setbacks, I keep in mind that life goes on. Is every day full of rainbows and sunshine? No. Far from it. Do I still get depressed? Sure. Do I still think "the unthinkable"? I hate to say it, but yes. It's part of my life. Part of the disease. I just don't let it consume me. I don't let it become me. I am more than my disease. I am more than a statistic. I remind myself that there are people who care about me. I remember that I've touched people's lives and I *do* make a difference.

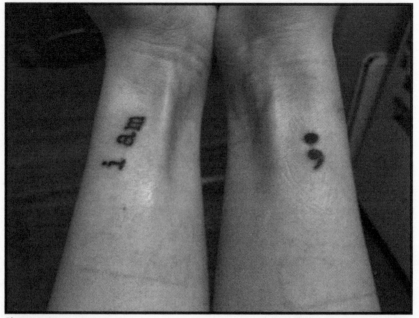

Christina M.

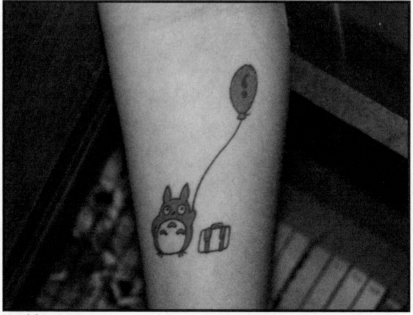

Magdalena D.

Anime has been a big part of my life since puberty struck (it helped me during that quite exhausting time), in particular, the character Totoro, who's a spirit, and only reveals himself if he wants to, which reminds me of myself.

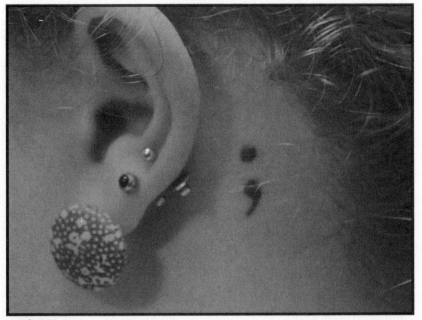

Heather F.

Danielle P.

RENEÉ B.

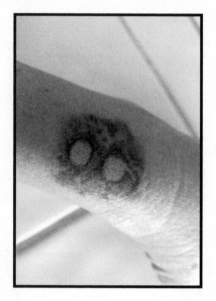

You have to remember that, just like with everything, it's all just temporary. Yes, the disease is forever, but your mood—bad, manic, or depressed—it's all temporary.

CHELSEA S.

There was no trigger, no huge event in my life I can point to and say, "That was the beginning." High school is tough for anyone, so I thought nothing of it. But soon what seemed like normal pressure for everyone else was becoming too much for me to handle.

It was like my head was in the clouds. Not my body, just my head. And I couldn't see clearly, but I could look down and see everyone else in the clear. School became harder, my concentration was nonexistent, sleep was the only thing I could do, and I didn't care if I had friends or not. I wanted to go to sleep and never wake up. There was so much sadness inside of me, I had to get it out. I tried art; that didn't work. I tried writing; that didn't work. The only thing that made me feel better was cutting myself and letting the pain drip out.

I knew it was wrong. I went to my mom at two a.m. one morning and told her I needed help. She hugged me and said okay. I am very lucky to have the support of my family, who realizes what depression can do to someone. Not only did I get therapy and medication, but my family was able to pull me out of a dark place. They allowed me to talk openly and get everything out in a healthy way.

Depression does not have a cure. I fight my bad days and celebrate the good days. Knowing that I am not alone, I am not crazy, and there is a light at the end of the tunnel keeps me going every day. I am motivated now to find my purpose in life and have wonderful experiences along the way.

I am not alone.

ACKNOWLEDGMENTS

You know how it is. You pick up a book, flip to the acknowledgments, and there it is: once again they forgot to mention you.

Not this time.

This book is for everyone who battles the symptoms of a mental illness and those who know all too well the stigmas that come with that. The shadows of mental health have consistently become more and more crowded. Every day, thousands of people find hope in a new, treatable mental illness diagnosis that explains the turmoils in their daily lives. Unfortunately, on those days and in those exact moments, someone decides to end their life because the darkness has become too much. This book aims to offer hope to those who are suffering in silence. Through a similar set of circumstances and a journey that resembles your own, we believe that you'll find a story that gives you the strength to continue;

this one's for you.

RESOURCES

There are many amazing organizations working to improve the lives of people suffering from mental illness. Some of these organizations are listed below. While all efforts have been made to ensure the accuracy of the information in the following sections as of the date this book was published, it is for informational purposes only. It is not intended to be complete or exhaustive, or a substitute for the advice of a qualified expert or mental health professional.

HELPLINES

Childhelp National Child Abuse Hotline offers crisis intervention, information, and referrals to emergency, social services, and support resources. 1-800-4-A-CHILD (422-4453) | www.childhelp.org/hotline

National Domestic Violence Hotline provides a vital link to safety for women, men, children, and families affected by domestic violence. 1-800-799-SAFE (799-7233) | www.thehotline.org

National Suicide Prevention Lifeline provides free and confidential emotional support to people in suicidal crisis and emotional distress twenty-four hours a day, seven days a week. 1-800-273-TALK (273-8255) | www.suicidepreventionlifeline.org

National Sexual Assault Hotline is part of Rape, Abuse & Incest National Network (RAINN), America's largest anti–sexual assault organization. 1-800-656-HOPE (656-4673) | www.rainn.org

Veterans Crisis Line provides confidential help for veterans and their families. 1-800-273-8255 (press 1) | www.veteranscrisisline.net

Crisis Text Line provides free and confidential emotional support to people in suicidal crisis and emotional distress twenty-four hours a day, seven days a week. Text START to 741741 | www.crisistextline.org

The Trevor Project provides crisis intervention and suicide prevention for LGBTQ youth. 1-866-4-U-TREVOR (488-7386) | www.thetrevorproject.org

COUNSELING AND TREATMENT

American Psychological Association: The APA's Psychologist Locator makes it easy for you to find practicing psychologists in your local area. http://locator.apa.org

Befrienders Worldwide is a dynamic and expanding global network of 349 emotional support centers in thirty-two countries across five continents. www.befrienders.org

Substance Abuse and Mental Health Service Administration: SAMHSA's Behavioral Health Treatment Services Locator is an online source of information for people seeking treatment facilities for substance abuse/addiction and/or mental health problems. www.findtreatment.samhsa.gov

SUPPORT GROUPS

Adult Children of Alcoholics exists for adults who grew up in alcoholic or dysfunctional homes and who exhibit identifiable traits that reveal past abuse or neglect. www.adultchildren.org

The Al-Anon Family Groups are a fellowship of relatives and friends of alcoholics who share their experience, strength, and hope. www.al-anon.org

Alcoholics Anonymous (AA) is an international fellowship of men and women who have had a drinking problem. Their primary purpose is to help people stay sober and help other alcoholics to achieve sobriety. www.aa.org

The Nar-Anon Family Groups are for relatives and friends who are concerned about the addiction or drug problem of a loved one. www.nar-anon.org

Narcotics Anonymous (NA) is an international, community-based association of recovering drug addicts. www.na.org

ADDITIONAL RESOURCES

Active Minds empowers students to change the conversation about mental health on college campuses. www.activeminds.org

American Foundation for Suicide Prevention (AFSP) exists to understand and prevent suicide through research, education, and advocacy. www.afsp.org

The Jed Foundation exists to promote emotional health and prevent suicide among teens and young adults. www.jedfoundation.org

National Alliance on Mental Illness (NAMI) is the nation's largest grassroots mental health organization dedicated to building better lives for the millions of Americans affected by mental illness. www.nami.org

National Eating Disorders Association supports individuals and families affected by eating disorders, and serves as a catalyst for prevention, cures, and access to quality care. www.nationaleatingdisorders.org

Self-Injury Outreach and Support (SiOS) provides information and resources about self-injury to those who self-injure, those who have recovered, and those who want to help. www.sioutreach.org